Maverick Cats

Maverick Cats

Encounters with Feral Cats

Ellen Perry Berkeley

Illustrated by Sandra Crawford

Walker & Company ☀ New York

First published in the United States of America in 1982
by the Walker Publishing Company, Inc.

Published simultaneously in Canada
by John Wiley & Sons Canada, Limited, Rexdale, Ontario.

ISBN: 0-8027-0714-9

Book design by Ganis & Harris, Inc.

Library of Congress Catalog Card Number: 82-40068

Printed in the United States of America

10 9 8 7 6 5 4 3 2 1

LIBRARY OF CONGRESS CATALOGING IN PUBLICATION DATA

Berkeley, Ellen Perry.
    Maverick cats.

        Bibliography: p.
        . Includes index.
        1. Feral cats. 2. Feral cats—Vermont—
Anecdotes.
I. Title.
        SF450.B47 1982   599.74   82-40068
            ISBN 0-8027-0714-9

for Roy
who has always known the important things

Contents

Paw Prints: An Introduction   8

On Names and Places   11

MamaCat, who started it all   20

On Mortality   25

The Honey Puss, who stayed as long as he could   30

On Territoriality   40

Turtle, who brought her babies   46

On Reproduction   53

Herbert, who never figured it out   58

On Predation   66

No-Name, who came to us to die   76

On Danger   81

Sylvester, who couldn't stay   88

On "Togetherness"   97

Turtle, who wouldn't leave   104

On Possibilities   117

Acknowledgments   127

Bibliography   131

Index   139

Paw Prints:
An Introduction

We'd had cats around the place for years, of course. Through the long winters, we saw their paw prints on every fresh snow—careful paths in and out of the carport, around and under the deck. But we rarely saw the cats themselves: only occasionally, on a gray morning, a wary creature staring at us from afar and then hurrying back into the brush or the woods.

Our house is on the south face of a very small mountain in Vermont. The land around the house was cleared—by us, and by the early settlers before us—but to the north, up the mountain, it is wooded. To the south stretches a broad valley of farms and fields. The cats live behind us in the woods. Or perhaps at the edge of the woods.

We'd seen only a paw print or a pair of eyes until one summer afternoon, when everything changed. A cautious young cat responded to Roy's coaxing and came up onto the deck. And because she decided, that sunny day, to let curiosity overcome caution, others in turn understood that they could do the same in safety. Over the next few years, five more cats came out of the woods and onto our hillside, sharing some part of their lives with the two human residents of this sunny slope.

I have written their stories: their small major dramas and grand minor sagas about attachment, departure, illness, mortality, danger, connection, growth, recovery, and need. The individuals and the events still haunt me, partly because of what I have experienced in this strange and moving interaction between wild animals and the people they chose to trust, and partly because of what I have seen of the world these animals know so keenly and we humans know so slightly. This is the world of the woods, where survival is a constant preoccupation and where safety is found only in small pockets—tiny folds—of time and space.

These are *feral* cats, defined most easily (too easily) as domestic cats living in the wild. I called them feral before I knew what the word meant or, more precisely, before I knew what it meant to all the people using it. There are several definitions of the word, and more than several other words for my definition. But the complexities only came later, when I sought more information about these animals.

I wanted to know everything about them. Where do feral cats come from? Are they born in the wild, generation after generation, or does a single animal wander off into the wild (or get dumped there) and die before reproducing? Are there many of them? Are they everywhere in the world? What are their lives like: long or short, easy or difficult? What do they die of? Which animals do they prey on? Which animals prey on them? Are they solitary or sociable toward each other? Do they have much contact with cats that are still domesticated? Do they have much contact with people? Are they dangerous to people? Do they ever become redomesticated? Are they considered pets or wildlife, or something else? Does anyone care about them? Has anyone seriously studied them? What attitudes do they arouse—are they hated, feared, pitied, loved, ignored? Are there official policies toward feral cats? Should there be? Are there unofficial policies, advocated or carried out? Should there be?

I asked a lot of people. Game biologists, veterinarians, specialists in animal behavior, humane societies, wildlife agencies—all the people concerned with pets and pests and evolving creatures and endangered species. I did a lot of reading. Sad little stories in the cat magazines and the animal-welfare newsletters. Unemotional accounts, full of grams and hectares, in the scientific and professional journals. And books giving feral cats a few pages, sometimes more: books by eminent researchers, books by everyday cat lovers, books by dog lovers who claim to have nothing against cats, and books by bird lovers who have everything against cats— everything but the facts.

In all my digging, I found no comprehensive, up-to-date, even-handed, and accessible discussion of feral cats—nothing available to people who are beyond the reach of obscure journals and private newsletters. But I found an active interest in these animals coming from several directions: from people concerned with animal behavior, who are trying to study domestic cats in as natural a situation as possible; from people concerned with the balance of nature, who are trying to measure the impact of feral cats on their environment, especially on any threatened species in that environment; and from people concerned with animal "control" and animal welfare, who are trying to prevent more cats from becoming feral and—in the dubious delicacy of our language about death—are "removing" those cats already feral.

I found a lot of material, all of it interesting, some of it disturbing. What I did not find were ready answers to my questions. The more I inquired, the more variety I found among the answers. Some questions *have* no definitive answers, I am forced to admit, either because the research has yet to be done, or because our attitudes toward all the animals of the earth— complicated and conflicting attitudes—have yet to be resolved.

But I'd had unanswerable questions of a different sort even before I looked beyond our hillside. I'd discovered with some pain that we could know "our" feral cats, our wild Vermont creatures, only up to a point—well enough to tell their stories, but well enough, too, to see these stories only as fragments of their lives. And as fragments of the richness of life in a New England woods.

So for those who love cats, for those who are curious about feral cats, and for those who do not mind some unanswered questions, I have written about the few animals we came to know personally, and I am passing along the observations and opinions of many other people, who have known many other feral cats.

On Names and Places

I had heard the word "feral," and used it, before I ever saw it on a page. I thought it meant "gone wild," and I was right, as far as I went. Then I went to our dictionary, a determinedly thorough volume under which are pressed the important flowers that mark the important occasions we can no longer recall. Here is the three-part definition of feral: "1. existing in a natural state, as animals or plants; not domesticated or cultivated; wild. 2. having reverted to the wild state, as from domestication. 3. of or characteristic of wild animals; ferocious; brutal." Each part of this definition is appropriate—more or less— to the feral cats I am writing about: the domestic cats "gone wild." These cats exist in a more or less natural state; they have reverted from a more or less domesticated state; and they are more or less like wild animals.

To confuse the matter, the word feral is often used for all the wild cats—lions, jaguars, cheetahs, bobcats, etc. I have seen this usage in various books, and in personal communications from people in such diverse callings as zoo management, wildlife conservation, cat genetics, and the cat fancy. (To the American Cat Fanciers Association, for instance, "a Feral Cat is a 'wild cat' or the progeny of a wild cat crossed with a domestic.") I mention this inclusive use of the word feral in order to put it aside, and to say quite clearly that tigers and wildcats, Safari cats and mountain lions, are not the subject of this book.

To confuse the matter further, the word feral has still another meaning, so different that it gets another entry entirely in our dictionary, not merely a new number in the same entry. This word is not the same word (although it *looks* the same); it comes from an altogether different root. Here the definition is in two parts: "1. causing death; fatal. 2. funereal; gloomy." I mention this secondary set of meanings only to discard it. If we were discussing ships, we would carefully diagram the bow of a boat, but we would not spend a moment choreographing the bow taken by a concert pianist. Let us return to the primary set of meanings for feral—the three-part definition that applies to so many familiar domestic animals.

I have read of feral swine, feral horses, feral cattle, feral camels, feral sheep, feral goats, feral donkeys. The plight of feral burros in the Grand Canyon has recently been in the news. The rampaging of feral dogs is sometimes a front-page story. Even our own species is said, on occasion, to live a feral existence. Psychologists and anthropologists use the term "feral children" (or "wolf children") for the children who are raised outside the human community, among wild animals. A television program coined the term "feral people" for the individuals who live on sidewalks and in subways, their meager belongings stuffed into shopping bags.

With an idea of ferality in general—"gone wild," for short—let's look at the feral cat in particular. Or rather, let's look at how various people look at the feral cat. Some say simply that the feral cat is "living in the wild" or is "surviving on its own without human aid." I have also heard the awkward term "self-fending."

Some observers place special importance on food. Two researchers in Australia define feral cats as "those field- or bush-roaming domestic cats that are forced to secure their own food." (Some of the cats seen by Brian Coman and Hans Brunner traveled considerable distances to secure household scraps as part of their food. No matter; they are still feral animals.) Many others use this definition. But what of the rural cats everywhere that are "owned" yet expected to find their own food? They are *not* feral animals. They go by the name of "preying cat," "hunting pet," "barn cat," "semi-domesticated cat," "semi-wild farm cat" and "free-ranging farm cat." (Often, I suspect, they have other names as well: Whiskers, Boots, and all the rest of it.)

Because food is an uncertain indicator, some people prefer another definition altogether for the feral cat. Roger Tabor, working with feral cats in Greater London, believes the term shouldn't depend on "whether a cat is fully supporting itself on caught food" but "should be used, as it is with other animals, for cats that have reverted from a domestic to a free-living state." ("Free-living," incidentally, is not the same as "free-roaming" and "free-ranging," which involve a human home to be let in and out of—or, at the very least, a barn to take shelter in.)

What, then, of the cats of the Portsmouth dockyard? Jane Dards believes they are feral, "since they are not domiciled with man." But the ten thousand people working at the dockyard provide the cats with food and shelter (boxes and bedding), quite apart from what is available to the cats in terms of found food and found shelter. These are feral cats, surely; "very few are tame enough to be handled," says Dards, adding this last more as description than as definition.

"It is difficult to formulate a precise definition of ferality," states Tom McKnight in his *Feral Livestock in Anglo-America*. He poses nine questions about conditions that may (or may not) define ferality, and at the end of his list he states that a precise definition cannot be given because "zoologists have not reached a generally accepted conclusion" on these points. McKnight's definition does not answer his own questions, but it does quite well for his own purposes, and for ours: "Ferality is here considered in a broad sense; that is, a feral animal is one that was once domesticated, or with domesticated ancestors, but is now living as a wild creature. It is not under the effective ownership of humans, and does not receive protection, care, or food as a deliberate gift from man." McKnight's monograph (like this book) includes animals that are "truly feral" as well as animals that are in a less definitively feral situation. The line is hard to draw, especially when the cat—more easily than most animals—can jump back and forth across this line with relative ease.

For all our efforts at defining the term "feral," not everyone knows or uses the word. Whatever definition we can construct will have any number of other terms applied to it: "ash-barrel cat," "alley cat," "woods cat," "wild house-cat," "ex-domestic cat," and "outside cat." Some of these lack a certain precision, but people seem to know exactly what they mean—more or less.

What about the ubiquitous animal that goes by the name of "stray cat" (a. k. a. "vagrant cat" or "vagabond cat" or "cat between homes")? McKnight himself uses the terms "stray" and "feral" interchangeably, as do others. Feral animals, in fact, are often called "domestic strays." But a distinction is worth making. According to Graeme Nicholson of the British Veterinary Service, a stray is "a domestic animal that has left an enclosure and wanders at large and is lost," while a feral animal is one that has "escaped from domestication."

A feral animal is not, however, "undomesticated." This was the term proposed in 1974 by the national conference on the Ecology of the Surplus Dog and Cat Problem, and it seems wrongly applied to an animal that might better be described as "de-domesticated."

A feral animal, having once been domesticated, is not the same as a wild animal. A wild animal may *become* tamed—indeed, many infant mammals can be tamed—but the ancestors of a feral animal have already *been* tamed, through the process we know as domestication.

There is reason to believe that the cat was not deliberately domesticated; that, instead, it moved by itself into the new ecological niche offered by the new settlements of humans. The natural prey of the cats was attracted to these settlements, and the cats followed, says geneticist Neil Todd. It shouldn't be surprising, says Todd, that there are no skeletal features permitting an unambiguous separation between wild and domestic cats: "If the cat was only an uninvited but not unwelcome guest in the human community, there is no reason to expect it to be modified in any dramatic way. In fact, since tolerance of its presence was based on its continuing to function in a manner virtually identical to its wild progenitors (*i.e.* active predation), modification might have interfered with its acceptance."

But, Todd observes, the cat has undergone "behavioral and presumably genetic adaptations" to living among humans. Another specialist in cat genetics, Roy Robinson, spells out the three-part route by which the cat "would seem" to have been domesticated: 1) a persistence into adulthood of certain juvenile characteristics, encouraging dependency and curbing pugnaciousness; 2) a hormonal modification, particularly reducing the adrenal response; and 3) a reduction in brain size, "impairing the animal's sensitivity to uncongenial stimuli." These changes are the changes of many generations and are not undone overnight. We may say that the feral cat has "gone wild" or "reverted to the wild," but this is not the same as being a wild animal.

For my own purposes as well as the reader's, I need to summarize this discussion of ferality. First we have a dictionary that gives two different definitions for the word feral, only one of which is pertinent to our subject—and from that one we need to separate all the lions and tigers. Then we encounter various theories of ferality based on quite different criteria. In addition, we have many other words standing in for the word feral, however we may define it. Finally, we have considerable confusion between stray and feral—and between feral and wild. How can I summarize? I am tempted to say (with apologies to all, and special apologies to my weighty dictionary) that a feral cat is basically a cat "gone wild."

How do cats become feral? Sometimes their owners leave. "Where people have abandoned island settlements," write Fitzgerald and Karl, "cats have often persisted." Men and cats have gone to many islands—sealing and whaling, exploring, setting up weather stations. The men come and go. Some of the cats stay. Cats are also left behind in the steady depopulation of rural areas and desertion of marginal farms.

Not only in conditions of hardship or in primitive settings are cats left to their own devices. A recent article in the campus newspaper of a Massachusetts college town tells of the annual rise in the number of animals that must fend for themselves when students leave for the summer.

Sometimes, then, the humans simply walk away—or sail away or hitchhike away. A more deliberate abandonment occurs when people drop their cats at a "dumping" spot. This place may be in the center of town (in Athens, it is the National Gardens), or it may be in the countryside. Five million dogs and cats are abandoned each year in the United States, according to the Department of Agriculture.

Sometimes cats are released with the blessings of government. Wally Davies and Ralph Prentice, writing about feral cats in Australia, mention that in the 1880s "thousands of cats were released away from settlements to help control the exploding rabbit population."

It isn't always humans who initiate the separation. "Cats are abandoned by people and people are abandoned by cats," as McKnight neatly puts it. I am told by the Department of Natural Resources of a southern state that feral cats "probably come not from abandoned pets but from pets that are still part of the household and are generally free to roam at will." This view is not uncommon. A wildlife biologist with the Department of Environmental Conservation of a northeastern state suggests that the practice of feeding pets outside may "help subsidize the tendency for urban cats to go feral."

A staff member of the Animal Protection Institute gives me an extraordinary figure: "A California survey has revealed that about 60 percent of the unaltered household cats will become feral in three years. Such cats reportedly leave of their own volition." I learn later about a California survey—almost certainly the same one—with 66 percent of the cats in a sample of households in Alameda and Contra Costa counties no longer in the household after three years. Nearly half of the cats had been given away, it turns out, but that still leaves 36 percent unaccounted for. Can so large a percentage of household pets be turning feral?

To "own" a cat is often considered dubious enough to require quotation marks, as though the cat can't—or won't—be owned. But the ties may be thin in both directions. According to the Pet Food Institute, 59 percent of cat owners are ranked "low involvement" owners; they have cats only because cats are perceived as needing little care and making few demands. Perhaps some of these cats respond to a low-involvement situation by departing. Surely some mismatches are terminated by the cat. Who can forget Booth Tarkington's freedom-loving Gipsy, suffocating in an excessively proper household, who "went forth in a May twilight, carrying the evening beefsteak with him, and joined the underworld"? Who can forget Mary Ellen Chase's "peculiar" Dolly Moses, an unloved animal whose "fits" catapulted her one Sunday dinnertime into the steaming soup tureen, and who then, in a fit of fear or embarrassment (or something else entirely), departed the house forever?

Sometimes it is an antagonism among cats that will drive one of them away. Many observers have written of the occasional cat treated as an outcast, a pariah, subject to all the aggressive attacks launched by others of its group. Who can blame such a cat for seeking its fortunes and foodstuffs elsewhere?

And sometimes the reasons are unknown. Writing about Macquarie Island, south of Australia, Evan Jones observes that the cats "had become feral" by 1820—ten years after the island was discovered and cats were introduced. The total adult population of feral cats on Macquarie Island is now estimated at 250 to 500 cats. Such cases can never be pinned down; enough to say that the people brought household cats, and either the people or the cats renegotiated the arrangement.

The Feral Cat Working Party (established in Britain by the Royal Society for the Prevention of Cruelty to Animals) lists no fewer than twenty-three situations causing a cat to turn feral. The situations range from accidental to purposeful, some caused by cats and some caused by people. These twenty-three "causes" are distinct from the bombing during World War II that produced feral cat colonies for the first time in British cities. The FCWP explains that "whole rows of houses were destroyed, families were evacuated and the domesticated cat found that it had to fend for itself."

Feral cats are fending for themselves almost everywhere in the world. "They apparently are not found in deserts," writes McKnight, "except in the immediate vicinity of human habitation or in irrigated areas. Desert summers seem to be more effective as a deterrent than subarctic winters." But feral cats exist in the deserts, too, at least in the Gibson and Tanami Deserts of Australia, according to a recent article by Jones and Coman. And even Alaska has its feral cats, although Pet Pride of Fairbanks tells me that there are very few "actual feral cats" in the interior and north of Fairbanks. "Odds are not in the cat's favor."

Yet feral cats live and multiply in fiercely inhospitable places. Marion Island, southeast of South Africa, is a volcanic protuberance approximately twenty kilometers in length, fifteen kilometers in width. The wind is ceaseless, and rain or snow falls three hundred days a year. On this strange piece of rock, several thousand cats have lived. They spent "most of their time" in subterranean lava caves, but in those parts of the island where natural refuge was limited, they took shelter in the burrows of petrels, their primary prey.

Feral cats are firmly lodged on many of the islands near Antarctica—on Macquarie Island, for instance, with its climate classified as "cold temperate or subpolar oceanic" and its temperature hovering just above freezing, summer and winter. The wind is strong, the precipitation is light but frequent, and the cloud cover is almost constant. Not a climate that a cat would choose.

In the most densely populated places and the most sparsely inhabited places, we can expect to find these animals. I have seen a feral cat on a platform at the lower-track level of Grand Central Terminal in New York City, and I have seen a picture of a feral cat photographed alongside an Australian road "some one hundred kilometers from the nearest human habitation."

"Many London squares," according to Roger Tabor, "have their own colony or colonies of feral cats." He feels that the word "colony" is appropriate since the cats do gather as a group, almost always where someone is putting out food. Does the feeder bring the cats together as a colony, he wonders, or does the colony cause a feeder to materialize?

Feral cat colonies throughout Great Britain have been exhaustively surveyed by Paul Rees, who found a total of 704 colonies and got detailed information on 287 of them. The most common habitats among the 287 are "hospitals, industrial sites and residential properties," but hospitals may be over-represented in this sample because hospital administrators were especially eager to help. Most of the 287 colonies are probably older than five years, and most have fewer than ten cats. Most (85 percent) are considered a problem in various ways, from "general nuisance" to "staff allergy." But almost half (46 percent) are considered a benefit, from "giving long-term patients a daily interest" to controlling rodents. Overwhelmingly (92 percent), these 287 colonies are fed daily by people.

Those who are best acquainted with feral cats, in fact, may well be the "cat ladies" who feed them (or even "cat gentlemen," as my friend Kristine writes from Rome). The Roman cats, of course, are legendary, peering out from behind the massive stones of Ancient Rome, sunning themselves amid the ruins. These cats are variously reported as "pathetic" and "quite literally starving" or "almost as fat as the obese white neutered cat that sleeps on the radiator in our pensione." Whichever it is, the cats are civil servants in their way, maintaining some control over the city's enormous rodent problem. (At times, the cats of Rome have given even greater service. Looking back to the lean years of World War II, it is said, "Before the war, we fed the cats; during the war, the cats fed us.") Interestingly, Rome's feral cats are now apparently leaving the center of town and heading for the outlying districts—too few cat ladies remaining in the built-up center, and too much noise and pollution.

Despite what the Feral Cat Working Party calls the "obsession" to feed cats, a good cat lady is hard to find. At Corona del Mar State Park in California, Mary George has fed her beloved "Beach Bums" daily for almost twenty years. During vacations from her other work (as a logistician), she hires a college student to prepare food for the twenty-five or so cats that live on these cliffs above the Pacific. Here, too, the cats are invaluable to humans, exterminating rats and cleaning up after the people who picnic and fish on the beach. The cats hide from strangers, but they know the sound of Mary George's car and run out to greet her.

It isn't only cat ladies who are interested in feral cats. Over the years, a fairly steady band of investigators has studied the foods eaten by feral cats, especially with an eye to the impact on game species. Still, by 1964, McKnight could say that feral animals were "almost completely disregarded by scientists and administrators" and were virtually ignored by wildlife managers.

By 1974 the national conference on surplus dogs and cats (sponsored, in part, by the two major private organizations, the American Humane Association and the Humane Society of the United States) expressed concern about the number of feral cats but said that "available data are inadequate to define the problems these animals may be causing." In 1979 two researchers in Tennessee found that all cats captured were adults, but didn't know what to make of this important finding because of "the total lack of information regarding reproduction and parental behavior of feral cats"—found, indeed, very little data altogether on the lives of feral cats, and that data mostly on food habits. To this day, the humane societies are not well-informed about feral cats. The Animal Protection Institute of America tells me that it is in the process of researching the general topic of feral animals, but that "we still do not know enough about feral animals to begin programs geared to assist and protect them."

Within the past five years or so, this situation has changed dramatically. In a variety of places, and for a variety of reasons, people have been studying feral cats: the "free-ranging" cats of the countryside, the "free-living" cats of the city, the "truly feral" cats of isolated islands. Whatever these people call themselves—zoologists, biologists, ecologists, animal behaviorists, sociobiologists, ethologists, environmental scientists—they have been observing, tracking, analyzing, measuring, counting, speculating on, and writing about the domestic cat gone wild. These studies on feral cats have been motivated by the need "to formulate informed policies on their management and control," as Evan Jones says about his four-year study of feral cats in southeastern Australia; by the "ethical as well as scientific" need to preserve a "sensitive and 'young' sub-Antarctic ecosystem," as Rudi van Aarde says about his long-term studies on Marion Island in the Indian Ocean; by the need simply to add to basic knowledge, because "the study of domestic cats as wild animals offers an unusual opportunity to advance understanding of mammalian social behavior," as David Macdonald says about his farm cats in rural England.

I will refer to these and other studies throughout this book. On four continents, studies have looked in sometimes excruciating detail (through radio-transmitted signals, through infrared binoculars, through computer-recorded data), at virtually the same animal I have seen, both more and less intimately, on our hillside in Vermont.

Mama Cat,

who started it all

We live in the southwestern corner of Vermont, technically in the town of Shaftsbury, but actually on the side of a mountain several miles from the center of town.

We are just north of Bennington, and in the winter, when the leaves are gone, we can see the obelisk in Bennington that commemorates the Battle of Bennington, fought in 1777 (and fought, incidentally, not in Vermont at all but just over the border in New York State). Our view throughout the year could be a page from *Vermont Life*: a wide and peaceful valley, placid cows, red barns, white houses. But the mountains purpling in the distance take the eye fifty miles into Massachusetts. The landscape has no state lines on it.

It was especially to Vermont, though, that we came. Our separate routes had taken Roy and me to New York City in the 1950s. We met there in the 1960s, and by the 1970s we were ready to move on. We didn't ski and we didn't plan to grow our own food, but we wanted to move to Vermont. Something about the land, the rolling hills, the space, the live-and-let-live ways of Vermonters. And so we found land and built a house, slowly shedding our lives in the metropolis and moving into new rhythms in the country. Our work remained the same: Roy is a writer, folklorist, historian, folksinger; he teaches, sings, makes records; I am a writer with a background in architecture. I write articles, give lectures, run workshops at architecture schools. The economic collapse of the magazine where I was a senior editor gave us the final push out of New York. It had been good there for us, but we were ready to leave.

We bought the land because of the view, and we camped on our acreage while we decided what kind of house we would build. Our backs were toward the mountain, not suitable to build on. Our eyes were toward the valley, not ours to build on. Woods behind us, grazing land below us. In between, a small plateau of once-cleared land: the place for our tent—and eventually our house.

Every new creature held our attention. A solitary hawk circling far above the treetops by day. A pair of whippoorwills calling to each other across the hills by evening. A restless layer of fireflies close to the earth by night. Our eyes were mainly on the view by day and the sky by night, and we didn't notice any ground animals—probably for the very good reason, too, that whenever we moved in for a weekend, with our tent and campfire and commotion, any animals headed for the hills. A four-footed *something* brushed our tent one drizzly night, but we let it move on and didn't try to identify it.

Once the house was up, though, and once the snows came, we looked out through double-thick windows to see the prints of many four-footed animals: deer coming down the mountain to browse among the bark and grasses that hadn't yet been stripped; rabbits making nervous loopy circles around the blackberry thicket; small rodents poking out from a brush pile. And cats. We couldn't tell whether it was one cat, tracing and retracing its path, or several cats, each following the path of the animal before it. Each cat—or the one cat—left only its path in the snow, and its scent for any animals who might follow. Each cat moved on.

But we knew they were there. And they certainly knew we were here.

During the summer, no glass separated us from the animals who also lived here. One warm afternoon on the deck, Roy glanced up from his reading to look directly into the eyes of a cat looking directly at him, not thirty feet away. He began to talk, chattering about how beautiful the cat was (not wholly true, but a harmless flattery) and how safe it would be for the cat to come closer. The cat came closer, all white and gray and suspicious.

"I wonder whether there's anybody inside," Roy cooed, not changing his voice, "who might bring out a morsel of food for this beautiful cat. Just a morsel. *Very* quietly. For a *very* beautiful cat."

I slipped outside with some hastily shredded pot roast, and she ate it, without gratitude, keeping her distance afterward as she padded slowly around the deck. She was pregnant, her unborn babies lying like saddlebags on one side or the other as she lay down, and shifting from left to right as she waddled.

We didn't expect much interaction from this dour and lethargic animal, and we didn't get much. But we kept feeding her, day after day, and she kept eating. She wasn't afraid of us, but she wasn't interested in us, either. We wondered when and where she would have the kittens.

She came around for several weeks, long enough to be named (MamaCat), but not long enough for much else to happen. We didn't want to make a "pet" of her, I hasten to say, or intrude on her. But, oh, hungry critters that we were, we could fairly taste the scrap of companionship she might toss our way. Alas, it was never tossed. Her lethargy, her disdain, were enlarging with her belly. The birth must be close.

Then, one evening, as we were wondering whether we would even know about the birth, we heard an insistent and high-pitched meowing from the place where the two wooden steps join deck to ground. Was she giving birth *here*? We hurried down from the second floor and peered out onto the deck through the kitchen door. But it was a different cat entirely! It was tiny, a weightless ball of honey-colored fluff, already a few months old. And not shy. It had jumped up onto the deck, and although it was startled by our sudden presence in the kitchen, it was not startled enough to run off. And soon it was drinking warm milk from its own bowl, snuggling into us afterward. Some minutes later, it wandered away into the soft Vermont evening, leaving us to smile at its outrageous insistence, its glorious independence, its touching need.

Thus began our acquaintance—no, our relationship, our involvement, our love affair—with the Honey Puss, who was really the first of our feral cats. I call them "ours," but I wouldn't say we owned them, unless I'd also say they owned us. Reasonable, perhaps, except that it is also unreasonable; nobody owns a cat, it is often said, but surely nobody owns a feral cat, no matter what the bargain. We simply "had" them: as eccentric friends, engaging companions, sly teachers, quick pupils, clever hustlers, unabashed seekers of affection. And they had us. They were "our cats" only in the intricate and reciprocal sense in which we were "their people."

MamaCat was really the first, but she lingered with us in such a languid way that I'm reluctant to say we "had" her at all—or she "had" us. She ate our food, and she lay on our deck, perhaps glad for this small measure of ease. But we stopped trying to interact with her, and she adorned the deck like another object, theoretically mobile but actually immobile: we had the porch chairs, the bird-feeder, the portable grill, and MamaCat.

She was disdainful now of the Honey Puss as well. He cringed at her petulant hissing, but he didn't seem to remember, from one minute to the next, that she gave him nothing but rejection. She was not his mother, we learned later. Surely he knew this, but he didn't seem to comprehend her notion of her boundaries, her need to maintain her separateness. He would tag after her, looking for a crumb of response or a snippet of food. Even after a full bowl of his own, he would nose speculatively into hers. She would glare at him, granting him a slow, silent, teeth-baring grimace. Or she would hiss at him, sending him another message that was oddly without body language behind it. And he would cringe and lay back—until it occurred to him to tag after her again and move in agreeably on her food.

Finally he gave up on her, content to follow her with his eyes alone. And she gave up on us, content to disappear completely. The free lunch hadn't been free enough. She must have had the kittens soon afterward, but we never saw a sign of them. Nor of her. Once I thought I heard them wailing, but it must have been the wind.

She was the first of our cats in an important sense, though, showing us how little we could know of their lives. Where had MamaCat come from? Where had she gone? Did she survive? Did the kittens survive? We would never know. Once I thought I saw one among the weeds, busy with some leaves. But I couldn't be sure. It may have been the wind.

On Mortality

If feral cats are elusive, the facts about them are even more so. On the statistics of life and death, little is conclusive.

A word about "facts." Throughout these portions of the book, I must often compare hunches with data, folk wisdom with solid research, the cries of passionate activists with the voices of calm observers. This is not merely comparing apples to oranges, but apple*sauce* to orange *juice* in some cases, so lacking in solid content is some of the material. I have done a great deal of searching, but definitive answers are often unavailable. In addition, of course, a definitive finding may not travel; the situation of a feral cat in one locale may be vastly different from the situation in another locale, in all the conditions of life and causes of death.

With this understood, I can proceed more comfortably. What is the life expectancy of a feral cat? The figures most often quoted are within a narrow range. A writer in the magazine *Cat Fancy,* for instance, states that "the average life of a stray cat is one to three years—if it is lucky." The head of staff at our local animal shelter thinks a moment and then says "in the wild, about two years, that's all." The anonymous author of a pamphlet explaining the federal Animal Welfare Act says that, of the millions of abandoned dogs and cats, "most die within a year." And the well-known writer on animals, Roger Caras, has written in the magazine *National Wildlife* that the average life span of dogs and cats lost or abandoned "isn't even two years." I questioned Caras about the source of this 1973 figure. "Largely folk wisdom," he replied, "although the age of dogs and cats collected as dead-on-roads (DOR) seemed to indicate a two-year median." He added: "I don't recall who did the grisly count or where." Would it matter? The DOR count will not include any feral cats who die far from human beings—or near human beings but far from roads. If the animals killed on roads are representative of all the animals out there, his figure is useful. Otherwise not. And this is anybody's guess.

Guesses are almost all we can get. The editor of the magazine *Modern Veterinary Practice* suggests that the life expectancy of feral cats is "probably much shorter than those at home," and he guesses 50 percent—which is probably no better or worse than any other guess. And some people refuse even to guess. Maurice Hornocker, the outstanding researcher on mountain lions, replies to my query about feral cats, "I have no idea of their life expectancy in the wild." But he also comments, "Feral cats are *cats*, and the cats are among the most efficient of all carnivores." They will do whatever is necessary to survive, says Hornocker, and it seems proper that he offers no actuarial table.

Occasionally there will be a legendary figure of a feral cat, old and indestructible. A woman answering a letter of mine in a newspaper remembers to this day a tomcat called "the Wild One." As a child, she saw it year after year.

I talked at length with our veterinarian, George Glanzberg. "A lot of the cats I see," he told me, "by age ten, are starting to have tooth problems, or other things that would make fending for themselves very difficult. Somewhere in the range of nine to fourteen years, I would guess, is where they can't take care of themselves in the wild anymore. I'm sure the mortality of young cats is very high, especially those born in wintertime. But mortality rate and age span are not necessarily related. If they make it to age two, they should be on a very healthy plateau for the next seven, eight, nine years." (By contrast, he says, many domestic cats live to "fourteen, sixteen, eighteen, twenty.")

From the biologists studying various cat colonies, we get findings specific to their sites. Near the Antarctic Circle on Kerguelen Island, for instance, where temperatures are very low and rains are almost constant, the oldest cats found were eight years old. The situation is hardly more favorable in the waters off Los Angeles; on San Nicolas Island, the Navy examined sixty-seven cats in 1980 and found only 4 percent it could describe as "old" (five or more years of age), the rest being 31 percent "immature" (under one year) and 64 percent "mature" (one to four years).

Mortality among kittens is indeed high. Rudi van Aarde of the Mammal Research Institute at the University of Pretoria has done extensive research on Marion Island, another of the islands near Antarctica where whalers, sealers, and meteorologists brought cats who later became feral. He has studied the feral cats in all aspects of their lives: their distribution and density, their reproduction and population ecology, their diet and feeding behavior. According to van Aarde, the mortality of kittens on Marion Island during their first two months of life is as high as 42 percent.

"Most of them die," Tom Wolski, veterinarian and animal behaviorist, told me in a matter-of-fact tone. We were walking the rolling farmland of Ithaca, New York, where he had been studying four colonies of farm cats—tagging more than a hundred cats, tracking many of them by radio, recording their travels and their vital statistics. The numbers are not pleasant to hear. Of all the litters born during the three and a half years of his study, only 50 percent of the kittens were alive at weaning; only 33 percent were alive at the age of one year. Wolski doesn't know the cause of death in one-third of the kittens not yet weaned ("unexplained disappearances" are 32 percent), but the two major causes he can identify are desertion or death of the mother (26 percent) and attack by dogs (18 percent). Other causes of death are minimal: disease (7 percent), automobiles (7 percent), miscellaneous (7 percent), and maliciousness (3 percent). His statistics change sharply for juveniles and adults of this free-ranging population. Again, he cannot explain the disappearance of one-third (34 percent), but 63 percent of the deaths are "automobile-related."

In Britain, the Feral Cat Working Party has obtained a broad view of feral cats, hundreds of them. Chairman of the FCWP, Oliphant Jackson, is the former curator of the animal division at London's Royal Free Hospital; he views the life expectancy of newborn feral kittens as "poor." Because they are "difficult to handle and impossible to treat," says Jackson, "many kittens die from feline diseases that are not recognized as being killer diseases." (Then, too, the nutritional standard is "sub-optimal.")

But "owned" cats—for whatever reasons—may not be long-lived either. A survey of households in Champaign County, Illinois, turned up one cat for every 9.9 persons. The age structure is interesting: "Almost one-half of the cat population consisted of individuals in their first year of life and just short of three-quarters were within the first three years of life." To the researchers, this finding suggests that "either the population is expanding rapidly or that many cats do not survive their first year of life." The contention of the researchers, published in 1977 in the *Journal of the American Veterinary Medical Association*, is the latter: that there is a high death rate among owned kittens.

Between birth and death, what is life like for unowned cats? We can't ask the cats, and observers disagree. *Collier's Encyclopedia* mentions that domesticated cats "frequently" turn feral and "seldom" return to domesticity: "The fact that such feral cats are usually well nourished and vigorous is an indication of the remarkable adaptability of the species." True, they are sturdy. The 1981 report of the Feral Cat Working Party refers to a "natural immunity" allowing feral cats often to recover spontaneously from all but the most desperate illnesses. And they make the best of what they've got. The free-living cats of the Portsmouth dockyard—three hundred of them—have been the subject of a comprehensive four-year study: "the first ecological study of urban feral cats to be undertaken," according to researcher Jane Dards. She reports that post-mortems on several cats showed them to be "in surprisingly good condition, with large fat deposits."

Feral cats are sometimes substantial in size. They can weigh up to twice the average weight of domestic cats, according to an article in *Wildlife in Australia* presenting the results of the 1977 Feral Cat Survey in Queensland. Earlier and elsewhere (in South America), Darwin himself observed that feral cats became larger and stronger than the stock they had left.

I attended a day-long seminar on cat genetics and spent the coffee break with the instructor, Neil Todd, a brilliant researcher on the population genetics of domestic cats, and director of the Carnivore Genetics Research Center in Newtonville, Massachusetts. "Cats don't need the kind of coddling they get," Todd said, and he explained that the populations "at large" are biologically more sound than the owned populations. Genetically, the healthiest cats are the least manipulated, according to Todd, although some of the individuals undoubtedly suffer. I didn't know what he was doing at this gathering of cat breeders who are seeking to create an ever more "perfect" show cat.

Many observers see the feral cat as having "a rough life." I had a long conversation with Ben Day, the director of wildlife at Vermont's Fish and Game Department. "The ones I've seen, it doesn't look like a day on the beach to me. I suspect many of them miss many meals, especially in the off-season. I suspect they have problems making a living." A woman at the local humane society uses the same phrase: "The more urbanized we get, the harder it is for them to make a living." (Only in civilized England has civilization perhaps eased the life of the feral cat; before the Clean Air Acts, notes biologist Roger Tabor, a cat had to work hard to pry open a metal garbage container and had to go through great quantities of ashes and cinders to get the edibles, damaging its teeth in the process. Now, with much of London "smokeless," a cat has only paper or plastic garbage bags to open and almost no ash to confront.)

Many see the feral cat as doomed to a pitiful plight, dying a miserable death from starvation, illness, poisoning, infirmity, predation, the elements; the list is long. Surely the life is hard. A veterinary practitioner spelled it out most eloquently at a symposium on "The Ecology and Control of Feral Cats" at the University of London in 1980: "They are tough and incredibly resilient in the face of adversity; in adversity that is a point in their favor. Against absolutely impossible odds it is a point against them, for surely their suffering is longer and more protracted."

The suffering of abandoned cats is depicted heartrendingly by the Friends of Animals. "Only one in a million abandoned animals escapes death from exposure, accident, or sadistic treatment," states one of its messages. The photo is clear, but the figure seems less than reliable.

In Defense of Cats provides a veritable catalog of cruelties, active and passive. Written by a former humane officer, the book tells story after story of the suffering of abandoned animals: some of it quite horrendous, some of it produced quite purposefully by people needing to commit an act of torture.

What constitutes cruelty? A wildlife biologist with the New York State Department of Environmental Conservation believes that "harboring 'barn' cats should probably be discouraged because it *may* be a form of cruelty." (In his experience, the cats are purposely underfed so that they will subsist on barn rats, and whole populations are periodically killed off by feline distemper.) A different view comes from a veterinarian, no less compassionate, just across the state line into Vermont. He says, "For five years, I've had a cat living in my barn. YellowCat does very well for himself. I give him milk occasionally, but the cat doesn't need me at all." I ask whether the cat lives a life of suffering, and the vet replies, in surprise, "No! Who've you been talking to?"

The people I've been talking to (and writing to, and reading), I must repeat, are often talking about widely different situations. In the face of diverse responses, based on diverse situations, it is difficult to sum up. But here is a somewhat balanced view, from Tom McKnight's excellent 1964 monograph *Feral Livestock in Anglo-America*: "The life of a stray cat is not an easy one. It is shot by hunters, run over by automobiles, chased by dogs, eaten by coyotes and bobcats and owls and hawks, subjected to severe weather that it is not really adapted to, and is prey to malnutrition and disease. But it is a stealthy and natural hunter with an adjustable appetite, and it can nearly always turn to man for food and shelter."

The Honey Puss,

who stayed as long as he could

He had appeared after dark, that summer evening, and we smiled as we watched him go off into the night, his belly full of warm milk. We wondered whether we'd see him again.

We needn't have wondered. The sun was barely over the hill the next morning, and we were still in bed, when we heard his steady meowing: the call of a very young but very determined creature. He wasn't demanding so much as yoohooing, and standing squarely on the deck where we would be sure to find him. We hurried to serve him, and for several mornings his control over the household was absolute; he meowing his readiness at about 6:20 A.M., and we responding as best we could at that hour.

After a few days, everyone relaxed. He would wait quietly, looking up at our bedroom window above the deck, and we would get up at our normal hour, serving him before we even popped a vitamin pill. He paced excitedly while one of us prepared his bowl. We talked to him through the screen door, and he talked back. But when the bowl was set down on the deck, he took only a sniff before trotting over to nuzzle up to us. Then, reacquainted, he was back at the bowl in earnest, tucking his hindquarters under him and sitting roundly at his food. I noticed that the cats in TV commercials don't sit at their dinners like this, don't celebrate their food.

But the Puss was developing special rituals of celebration. Just before Roy set the bowl down onto the deck, one paw went lightly onto the back of his hand. Roy began to wait for this each time, and the Puss began to accommodate each time.

"It's a trick he taught me," said Roy, proud of them both.

"He doesn't do that with me," I bristled. "You're encouraging him. Soon you'll have him performing for company."

Roy laughed. "Not so. It's a trick *he* taught *me.* Maybe he doesn't think you're smart enough to learn it!"

I laughed then myself, because I know that Roy considers me smart enough to learn almost anything. And because I consider Roy smart enough to know almost anything, I think he just may have been right. This little trick—this gentle paw on the hand—was always done with Roy, and was never done with me.

Sometimes we were ready with food before the Puss was ready with his appetite, and we'd whistle, as we always whistled when food came out. Now we'd see him trotting swiftly through our lawn of wildflowers, virtually running for the last ten yards. Food is food, make no mistake, and the whistling meant food. But the whistling also meant *us*, and he usually ran exuberantly to *us* before exploring the food nearby. He was clearly delighted to be whistled up, to be welcomed and fussed over. We were also delighted, of course, to be greeted this way. And we were awed that this creature—having the ability to survive in the wild—also had the where-withal for a "civilized" existence. We were awed by his sweetness toward us, his civility, his eager availability.

Was it difficult to find a name for this combination of characteristics? We didn't look for a name for him; "Honey Puss" just came out—part endearment and part description—calling up the full sweetness and wildness of honey itself. But friends called him Honey and felt awkward. We usually called him Puss to his face and referred to him as The Puss or The Honey Puss, and that seemed fine with all of us. He responded to the word "puss" (spoken with slightly rising inflection), but he responded to many things. Often we thought it possible that he knew a lot more than we thought he knew!

He always knew everything that was going on, and almost always insisted on being a part of it. Not a pest, simply a busybody.

We offered a few quiet activities. The Puss would lie across my midsection and arms as I relaxed on the deck, writing. He'd snooze there against my warmth, or play quietly with the plastic top of my ballpoint pen.

But he was on the alert for more spirited interactions, and he would leap to accompany us on our walks in the woods. Here he would act the most appalling show-off; he'd climb a few feet of tree just ahead of us, then look back to see if we were watching, then leave that tree and rush ahead to find another one to climb. He'd be more sedate on the open road, trotting along at our pace by weaving from left to right just in front of us. We had to be careful not to trip on him as he zigzagged across our less embroidered route.

For any special activity in the brush, he would materialize in a flash. Roy was removing a tent-caterpillar from a small tree and was startled by the sudden presence of the Honey Puss, soon halfway up the tree. When the tree snapped unexpectedly out of Roy's hands, the Puss was catapulted fifteen feet into the air. He landed on his feet—of course—and trotted back in good humor, possibly eager to repeat the stunt.

And when I planted tulip bulbs, I am certain that the Puss considered it a game designed expressly for his amusement. He kept stalking and attacking the paper bags; he kept threatening the pail of water; he kept digging at the holes I was making. I enjoyed his company immensely, that day, and I am pleased to think that he returned the compliment. During the few moments when he wandered along the driveway to continue his cavorting (with sticks, with grass, with unknown beings), I realized that he didn't usually play in the driveway this far from the house. He wanted to be near me! I was chagrined to think that we usually demanded his companionship on *our* terms, on *our* turf: on or near the deck. I decided to go with him more often to his territory.

But it was hard to know where his territory was, he was so often on ours. He was at home in our civilized setting (outdoors) and at ease with any people or vehicles joining us.

In fact, he was hugely drawn to cars. He would stand back—out of caution more than fright, it seemed—when a car approached. But a car come to rest was a ready-made plaything. He was satisfied to crawl up under a fender, or print his small muddy paws across a hood. But if a car door should open, he'd be inside in an instant, giddily exploring seat and floor and dashboard. This was fine with most visitors; a man who came with his partner to advise us about lightning rods spent an amicable half hour alone in his car with the Puss, to their mutual pleasure. But one friend, who had a strong aversion to animals, got out of her car to greet us and was horrified to turn back to the open car and find the cat inside. She tried to "shoo" him out by shouting at him and swatting a paper bag of car trash at him. Nothing doing. He was firmly settled on the dashboard, regarding *her* as the interloper. We showed her how it could be done; like the old Bogart movie, "all you have to do is whistle"—but you have to be courteous about it! The Puss came out immediately, and the friend registered such disapproval (of the cat, of us, of all this madness) that I invited her into the house only after a silent argument with my better instincts and only because she had driven two hundred miles to see us.

The Puss took to most strangers, even the ones who didn't take to him. People who knew cats were amazed to see one so sociable—so responsive to a whistle, so *talkative*—and were even more amazed that this one was born and bred (and still living) in the wild.

He undoubtedly had his special places out there in *his* territory, but it didn't seem quite cricket to look for them. We were aware of his favorite spots on our turf. He had his accustomed lookouts and shelters: special corners of the carport and deck, special points in the driveway and lawn. Some of them made sense to us, and some of them didn't.

The inside of the house was of little interest to him. He slipped in a few times, but followed us out again. Only rarely was it necessary to pick him up and drop him outdoors again, a lack of hospitality he accepted without offense. He seemed genuinely respectful of our perimeter; our place was ours and his was his. Never did he scratch at the door, and only once did he intrude on our upstairs domain, climbing the maple tree outside our bedroom window to check on us at an unusually late hour for his breakfast. (This was possibly the first tree he had ever climbed, for Roy had to spend the next fifteen minutes on the ground coaxing him down.)

He had a mother nearby, but she was busy elsewhere at such critical times. She was a *grande dame* of a cat, very large, extremely wary of people, and she consented to come up onto the deck only two or three times. On one of these occasions, Roy was able, very gently, to remove the flea collar that was deeply furrowing her handsome ruff. The collar must have been put on when she was much smaller, much younger. We knew nothing more of her early life. We called her Madame (accent on the second syllable), and we wished we could have known her better. But she kept her distance, and we saw her only a few times, once as she was waiting at the bend of the driveway to collect her little likeness and take him off with her. She had lent him to us, though, in a sense, by allowing him to spend so much time with us, and we knew a bit more about her because of that. She must have been nearby quite often, teaching him whatever it was she would be teaching him.

Civilized and amiable as he was, we could see the hunter instinct in him. It was often more potential than actual; we watched him stalk grasshoppers, pounce at leaves, lie in wait for . . . what? We never saw him make a kill. Perhaps we were not encouraged to see it. Yet his supermarket diet was surely supplemented by small furry animals; when he once vomited, we were presented with a partly digested stew of rodent parts that could not have issued from our kitchen.

In any case, when I first saw him poking at a tiny limp mouse, I made an absurdly big fuss, petting him enthusiastically. I didn't know whether he had killed it or just found it, but he didn't seem to want to eat it. It just lay there—a soft dead wad—until we picked it up with a paper towel a few days later and took it into the woods.

We came much closer to life in the wild, some weeks later, when we heard a terrible bleating from the carport and found a tiny rabbit, dreadfully torn and barely alive, but still conscious. Roy shoveled it onto a piece of cardboard, took it outside, and shot it. I was surprised to see him upset; he has hunted since boyhood. And he was surprised to see me relatively unaffected by the incident; I had seen little, before this, of the life and death of animals. Roy didn't want me to see this dying animal or to see its death. I went into the grass that afternoon to steal a look at the lifeless body, but it was already gone, carted away by another creature of the wild. My compassion for the victim was outweighed by my fierce exultation for the Puss; he knows how to do this, he can get along in the world. I was glad that we (and our catfood, canned and bagged) could not tame him. Romantic? Yes. But not foolish, I hope.

It seems both romantic *and* foolish to attribute human motivations and feelings to any other animal. We wanted simply to observe our feral cats, and to draw no conclusions or comparisons. Yet we came to identify in the Honey Puss what I can only call his "personality" (his "animality"?). We would sometimes return after an absence of several days, for instance, and find him voracious for our presence. He would rub against us, not leaving us alone, walking too closely in front of us, tripping us as we went. Was this expression of need so very different from that of a human being? Or he would lean into our caresses, eyes closed to slits or completely shut, mind and body drugged with (could it be?) happiness as we "scritched" him. Was this so very different from the sensual pleasure of a human being? Or he would try to resist the several large pills we were instructed to give him, pushing Roy's hand away, but with the claws *in* so as not to inflict damage. We found him gentle and honorable—more so than a good many human beings.

We got to know his ways, and we admired them—admired him. Never grumpy, never timid, never nervous. Unfailingly patient, hardy, agreeable. And I realized that his most admirable qualities were among the qualities I most admire in human beings: the ability to be tough but gentle, and the need to be affiliative but independent. I had never known cats before, but Roy (who had) considered the Honey Puss very special.

Not only because I loved him—the familiar distinctness of him—but also because he was beautiful, I loved to look at him. The fat little paws, soon adjusting their proportion to the growing animal. The tidy little mouth: a friend's daughter called him Smiley. The tufted ears: was he part bobcat? The elegant whiskers, occasionally bent or broken from some encounter we could only imagine. The proud bushy tail, unlike any of the feral cats we'd seen before. He had a lot of Maine Coon Cat in him, and maybe not much else.

I found his coloring a special delight: fur like honey, like caramel, like champagne; eyes like a different vintage of champagne. And touches of pink: his pink ears, pink tongue, pink footpads, pink anus. I marveled at the varied textures of his coat—the velvet on his nose, the fine sleek hair on his back, the matted fur on his stomach, the untidy wool on the backs of his hind legs and on his bottom.

He was fastidious by instinct, licking his paws and brushing his whiskers after every meal. But he often had leaves hanging from his bottom, especially when the season changed and the damp leaves were everywhere. And he had burrs matted into his belly fur, soon becoming such impenetrable knots that he gave up trying to bite them out. I was more patient, and one of our pastimes—the Puss and I—was the careful removal of these furry tangles of twigs and burrs. He was patient, too, during the grooming, but only if diverted by interesting conversation. And I was no match for Roy and his livelier games: the old crumpled-paper-on-a-string kept them both strenuously amused until Roy laughingly begged to be excused.

I mentioned conversation a moment ago, and you are perhaps wondering who talked to whom. Roy and I talked to the Puss—and the Puss talked back, volubly. He didn't talk *only* to us, I should add, but kept up a running discourse with anything that crossed his path. "What a little character," Roy laughed, as he watched the Puss chattering at weeds, muttering at grasshoppers, bragging at pebbles. Sometimes, to be sure, the Puss must have been silent, stalking some delicacy. But I wonder whether his dialogues with such "noncommunicative" partners as the insects and the flowers weren't another form of my dialogues with him. We were not exchanging Great Ideas, he and I, but we were in good contact, and each of us got across a few basic points of view. Each of us (I am certain of this) considered it time well spent and time enjoyed.

He had many other special ways. We celebrated the alertness with which he attended to the "little noises" long ago screened out by our own ears. (Sitting on the deck, we could tell when the teakettle was nearing its boil by the attentiveness the Puss was directing toward the house.) We celebrated the delicacy with which he added his wastes to the soil, permitting only Roy to see him in this act. We celebrated the flatulence— sometimes an excessive performance—with which he amused or embarrassed our guests. And always, we celebrated his sociability; if one of us began talking on the phone, absentmindedly looking out through the screen door, the Puss would suddenly appear on the deck to engage in *his* part of the conversation.

He was maturing. He began to explore places beyond our whistle-call and to disappear for hours, even days. Still, when we had to abandon *him* for a day or two, and we looked back at him standing motionless in the driveway and watching us depart in the Jeep, I felt that we were all suffering.

It was on our return from a two-day visit with friends that we knew he was ill. He was languishing in a corner of the carport, too dispirited to greet us and too ill to have eaten the food we had left him. We checked him for bruises or wounds, and he seemed unhurt—just ailing and feeble, and crying mournfully with each breath: a special cry of misery we hadn't heard before.

An infection, said the vet, and a fever. "And he's got a tapeworm," she said briskly, flicking some ricelike particles from his woolly bottom. She was less professional—I would even say she was aghast—to learn that we occasionally dumped a live mouse from our basement Havahart traps into the general vicinity of the Puss outside. Aghast not so much because he got the tapeworm from such creatures (the ones from our basement and the ones he got on his own), but because . . . well, it wasn't exactly what the Havahart folks had in mind.

She was also reproachful about his name: "too soft and gentle for a tough tom," she said firmly, writing HONEY on the envelope of pills. (Alas, I thought, one more liberated woman who can't imagine a liberated man.) We guessed later that the full name, in her files, was probably HONEY BERKELEY, and we didn't like that either. He isn't ours, we protested to each other; we're just keeping company together for a while.

Before we left the vet's office, she spoke about having him "fixed." (What a regrettable euphemism, with its unspoken "that'll fix you!") She was giving us the best and latest advice: it would be for his own good, to keep him from getting into scrapes with other toms and having constant abscesses from his wounds.

But we thought of all the city cats we'd seen—most of them "fixed" for the convenience of their owners and some of them declawed, made defenseless, for the same purpose. If he's living as a wild animal, we asked ourselves, why can't we leave him with his wildness? (We understood later that this is a far more serious matter than we had realized. The vet hadn't mentioned the vast number of offspring this one tom might produce, and there was much else we didn't understand.)

Especially after he became acquainted with Turtle, a nervous young tortoiseshell who appeared at his bowl one day, we knew we wouldn't have him neutered. He wasn't sure what to make of her at first, but whenever she approached he retreated to the farthest corner of the deck, looking at her with wide eyes. I expected him to be more assertive, but Roy reminded me that the Puss was still essentially a kitten, and smaller than Turtle; perhaps they'd already fought it out and Turtle had established dominance, Roy said.

Then we watched them negotiate a new arrangement. The Honey Puss was suddenly much larger and stronger than before, his infection and tapeworm gone. He had become a handsome, leonine young tomcat. He began to sniff cautiously at Turtle, and we saw him reach out softly once, as if to caress her. "Don't be silly, that's so anthropo*morph*ic," said a young friend, newly graduated from a prestigious college. "I'm not so sure," I answered. "If he reaches out to touch us that way, why shouldn't he do the same with her?" Once, too, Turtle and the Puss seemed to kiss, their mouths coming close for a long instant. "I don't *believe* it; you're making it up," said my young friend, and I was taken aback by her tone of accusation, of certainty. What could be so unthinkable about blurring the lines between human beings and animals? Well, I had graduated from a prestigious college myself, and I remember what a closed community we were, a breed apart. . . .

Sometimes, too, we would see Turtle and the Puss wander off together down the driveway, companions of a sort, whatever else was happening between them. Once, when they came into view again, down at the road, we saw the Honey Puss climbing a tree ahead of her, then rushing further ahead to find another tree.

Until now we wondered how he would cope with our occasional absences; now we wondered how we would cope with his—perhaps even his permanent departure. We would worry; we would grieve. And we would miss this engaging fellow.

We didn't know how much, though, until it happened. We were away from home for several days in late November, and he left during that time. We could only hope that he left in good health and good spirits, but we had no way of knowing. The vet had warned us that he would disappear for days, establishing his territory, and we hoped that this was the case.

Nevertheless, I suffered a brief guilt. Had we failed him in some way? "No," said Roy, "it's just his way. We have to accept it. And even celebrate it. He's following his destiny. . . . Nobody owns a cat."

Still, though, we tried to whistle him up a hundred times during the next weeks. We looked in vain for his tracks in the new snow. "It's Nature's way," said Roy, comforting us both. "But I loved him so," I wailed, aware that this was not a rejoinder to his explanation. "You can still love him," Roy answered. We both felt desolate, bereft, older from this rite of passage.

In time, we missed him less. We accepted the likelihood that it was all about territory—perhaps the cat who had fathered him was in this area, or some other rival—and, in fact, months later we were regularly visited by a large and healthy male cat, a lardy and sober fellow we called Herbert. (But that is another story.)

We also accepted the likelihood that even the least lively barn in the area would be a more attractive winter resort than our carport. "My money's on *him*," said Roy. "He's either staked out a new territory or he's found some new folks to stay with. Nobody that keen and resourceful has to be worried about."

We worried a little about Turtle, though; she, too, disappeared during the long winter. She reappeared almost a year later with two tiny kittens, one of them bearing a strong resemblance to the Honey Puss. (That, too, is another story.)

When I began writing about the Honey Puss, I thought that the story would end here, with his disappearance and our uncertainty. But the story has no such ending, and I don't know that it ends with this next episode either. Fully a year later—again in November—Roy was looking down from the second floor and saw the Puss (unmistakably the Puss) making a quick inspection of the deck. "But by the time I got down there," said Roy, "he was gone." Roy was baffled more than sad.

In a way, I find this recent encounter—this near-encounter—more poignant than his long-ago need for us and accommodation to us. He doesn't remember us now, doesn't need us, doesn't recall the language of our life together. He was ours for a while. And we were his. But he's grown now and all is different. And so it must be. It's Nature's way.

On Territoriality

That was six years ago. Two years ago, and two miles from our home, we saw the Honey Puss again. He was in a field, far back from the road. It made sense. He had left our hillside to seek his own place, and he had come this distance. He'd have gone a greater distance if he'd had to, but not *unless* he'd had to. In his way, he knew what it meant to be "territorial." And when I came to know what it meant, in my own way, a lot of things made sense.

One of the outrageous fictions we have invented about animals living in the wild is that they are free to roam at will, settle at random. The truth is at once less romantic and more remarkable. Animals are not free. They restrict themselves to well-defined territories. They defend and use these territories (and, in fact, stay or leave altogether) according to precise rules for their species, their sex, their age.

The meaning of territory to any species can often illuminate the whole social organization of the species. This is why the territorial behavior of so many different animals has been so intensely studied. The feral cat has only recently joined this group, but it is already possible to look at the familiar creature we call the domestic cat and see in its territoriality as a free-living animal a fascinating new dimension. We can no longer call the feral cat a "vagrant," as if it had no home. It *has* a home—but not with us. Indeed, feral and rural cats are so ruled by territorial behavior that, as Neil Todd writes, "these cats probably live their entire lives not far from their place of birth."

Early conjecture on feral cats and territory was concerned with distance rather than behavior. In his 1940 study of rural cats in Oregon, Nils Nilsson stated with some hesitation that "feral cats travel at least twice as far as farm cats, and that male farm cats travel twice as far as female farm cats." A decade earlier, Aldo Leopold thought it probable that the feral cat, "harder pressed for a living," might have a cruising radius greater than the four miles observed for a non-feral cat.

That was that, until the 1950s, when the German ethologist Paul Leyhausen wondered what kept a population of solitary animals in contact with each other, rather than separate from each other. He was not the first to suggest that territory must have a maximum as well as a minimum size, but how was it maintained? To explore all this, Leyhausen and his colleague Rosemarie Wolff attempted "an uninterrupted, continuous day-and-night record" of three farm cats. Leyhausen later admitted that the task was impossible; one cat alone would have required "at least three well-trained, physically fit, and inexhaustible observers, plus a lot more equipment than we could command at the time." Together, Leyhausen and Wolff had data on only one of the cats—incomplete data at that—and they published this "only reluctantly" in 1959. But on the basis of their other observations of free-ranging domestic cats (urban, suburban, and rural), Leyhausen presented a picture in 1965 that he felt "quite confident" was "correct in its essentials."

Individual cats, writes Leyhausen, "own a territory which tallies roughly with Hediger's description of the average mammalian territory"—basically a "first-order home," plus a "home range" consisting of additional places that are regularly visited and are connected by an elaborate network of paths. Areas enclosed between the paths are virtually unused.

Neighboring cats will often use the same network of paths and the same hunting grounds and other sites, says Leyhausen, but "common use normally does not mean simultaneous use," and he describes the behavior of two cats approaching a "cat crossroads." They will sit and stare at each other, looking deliberately away from time to time. Eventually one cat will move hesitantly toward the crossing while the other is looking away, and will proceed hastily across it. Or both cats will move back almost simultaneously in the direction they came from. Only rarely will a fight occur (when the confrontation is sudden and unexpected), but any later confrontations between the two animals will usually end in a chase, not a fight.

Perhaps most interesting is Leyhausen's formulation of two types of hierarchy. The ranking that develops from clashes over territory is only a *relative* hierarchy, not valid at all future times and locations for the animals involved. The ranking that develops from fights between tomcats, however, is an *absolute* hierarchy, valid in the future for the two animals "at all times, in all places, and under all circumstances."

Leyhausen's work inspired others. He had noted that domestic cats, because of the changes of domestication, have become "less repulsive" to each other, "and in most cases can be brought to share a home area and even a first-order home." John Laundré, a young biologist in the Midwest, had grown up with farm cats and had long known that the domestic cat "seems to favor a solitary existence in the feral state but will live communally to utilize a common food source," as he wrote in 1977. Laundré found little evidence of spatial territoriality among his study group of ten farm cats. He found much overlap in the use of areas, for instance, and no defense of these areas. (Perhaps he was defining "spatial territoriality" too tightly for these easygoing animals.) He found no indication of temporal territoriality: the use of the same area by different animals according to a fairly strict timetable. (Leyhausen had seen this only in caged animals, but thought it *could* occur in free-ranging.) The conclusion drawn by Laundré was that the milk given the cats at milking time, drawing together a related group of individuals, "could reduce strong territorial behavior." It was a beginning. But there was much that Laundré couldn't see. The cats were lost to him whenever they disappeared into woods or tall grass—or darkness. He is now doing more sophisticated research on the use of habitat by farm cats, using telemetry.

Telemetry is simply measurement from afar. In biotelemetry, sensors are attached to an animal (or swallowed by it, or implanted in it), and a receiver near or far picks up life signals, such as heartbeat or respiratory rate. In "radio tracking," an animal's position is found and followed by means of a directional antenna that picks up the signal emitted by a transmitter on the animal. Radio tracking can be considered a *kind* of biotelemetry, although it is also said to *combine* occasionally with biotelemetry to give both locational and physiological data.

Radio tracking has been in use only since 1963, but it has virtually revolutionized wildlife studies. And the field is booming: new devices, new studies, new animals. Who knows what may come next (full audio and video are not unimaginable), but even the lowly "beep" has brought intriguing results. One of the primary uses of radio tracking thus far has been in the study of territory, and the territorial behavior of the free-ranging cat is already known to us far better than Leyhausen could have dreamed when he was scrambling after those three farm cats.

An important study has recently been completed in England, in rural Devon. The subjects: a family of four farm cats (plus a fifth born during the study). The researchers: Oxford zoologist David Macdonald and graduate student Peter Apps. For almost a year, Apps lived among the cats—he in a cabin ten by fourteen feet, they in the farmyard. The cats were fitted with miniature radio transmitters, each painted the color of the cat to keep the cat from attracting the attention of other animals. The men were equipped with a portable antenna, infrared binoculars, and a sophisticated electronic device called an "event recorder," into which they could instantly punch the full information on all cat interactions. The result is what Macdonald calls "a detailed sociogram of this colony," to be compared with colonies of other sizes and in other habitats. A further result, of course, is a detailed outline of each cat's movements. The cats stayed mostly around the barn during the day but traveled farther at night, the male covering about sixty hectares (and several farms), the three females covering from two to seven hectares (and only one farm). Each cat had its exclusive areas, but their home ranges "overlapped widely."

A tenfold difference between male and female home ranges was also recorded by Jane Dards at Portsmouth dockyard. This was not a job of radio tracking, but of many sightings of 119 cats plotted on large-scale maps and then calculated to avoid the distortions of too easy a computation; after all, the cats travel on paths, to sites, and do not recognize "areas" within "boundaries." Here the home ranges are much smaller than in Devon. The ranges of the males overlap extensively, as do the ranges of females (most of whom live in family groups and share their ranges with other adult females). "This social grouping in an animal usually considered to be solitary," says Dards, "is probably an adaptation to a favorable environment"; the dockyard has concentrations of ample food and shelter. She notes that excessive inbreeding is prevented by the large ranges of the toms and by the emigration of new toms into other parts of the dockyard. Some young toms remain with their original group, but they "do not show any of the characteristics of mature males," and they range over an area comparable to an adult female's range.

The tenfold ratio of male-to-female range is true even in central London, according to Roger Tabor, although the size of these home ranges is far smaller than at Portsmouth dockyard. The small size is only possible, says Tabor, because of the "superabundance of food in urban areas," mostly from human feeders.

"Area doesn't mean anything, talking about range," Tom Wolski told me. "Distance and overlap might mean something." Wolski has been studying free-ranging cats in the vicinity of Cornell University as his doctoral research in animal behavior. We met in Ithaca one morning after he had spent all night running across the hills, directional antenna in hand. Wolski, too, has found the male range to be far more extensive than the female range, extending to three or more farms, and "most nights" the tom covers the whole range. "He doesn't *need* to eat in all those places. He's doing it to keep other toms from his females."

Wolski has observed that the one dominant male on each farm overlaps the lesser males and females, while these overlap each other. Females sometimes leave their territory after weaning a litter, although this is unusual and "unselfish" behavior. Most young males emigrate, "presumably to get away from their fathers." Wolski hasn't found more than an occasional example of Leyhausen's temporal territoriality. "Small portions of adjoining ranges may be shared by pairs" on a kind of "time-plan basis," one cat following the other by several hours or a day and the two never meeting. In general, both males and females "keep regular, even rigid schedules." Yet change is constant and swift; when a cat dies, its range is usually taken over within a week. I asked Tom Wolski what surprised him in all these discoveries, and he was quick to answer, "that they *are* as territorial as they *are*."

In southern Sweden, spacing patterns have been recorded in detail—by direct observation and by radio tracking—as part of a long-term study of a population of rural domestic cats. (About 10 percent of the population was defined as feral, not fed regularly at households.) Olof Liberg of the University of Lund has outlined the findings of the four-year study. Females live alone or in groups around human households. Within each female group, home ranges overlap "almost completely," while neighboring female groups have "little or no overlap," even when the houses are close enough to make overlap possible. The females leave vast areas unused, seldom venturing farther than six hundred meters from the home farm. A few males—usually the feral males—have "large, evenly distributed home ranges that together covered most of the area." The male ranges overlap "moderately."

Most females in Liberg's area remain all their lives in the places where they were born, although a few move to new households—"invariably" to households without other females. Most males don't stay where they were born, even though their household offers secure food and shelter. Liberg suggests that "young tomcats leave the protection, and sometimes the affectionate love, of their owners" because of competition for mates. Male cats go through a sequence of life stages—from Novices to Outcasts to Challengers to Breeders—with the various stages marked by distinct behavior in their use of space and in their relationships with each other. The Outcasts, for instance, minimize their contact with the dominant males by dispersing, usually assuming a feral life.

Liberg raises many complex questions about density, adaptation, and hierarchy. I find myself wondering, in addition, why only one of these seventeen feral cats was female, why she used an area "much larger" than domestic cats "usually do," and why the domestic males were "subdominant" to the local feral males.

We don't know many things. Liberg concludes by saying that while "some evidence points to territoriality as a cause for spacing and dispersal, both in males and females," the picture is "somewhat contradictory."

We don't know *why*, and we barely know *what*. We do understand that feral cats around the world live at different densities, under different conditions, and in different relationships to human provisioning. We can only speculate on the effects of these and other variables on the powerful force of territoriality.

We know a few things, though. In a paper by Dards about the cats at Portsmouth dockyard, I was touched to read that "female cats are apparently very reluctant to leave the areas in which they are established. One group of cats continued to live in and around a building while it was demolished and rebuilt." It wouldn't be our food, then, that would keep Turtle, the timorous and appealing tortoiseshell, on our hillside. Feeding her would not be necessary to keep her in residence on this piece of ground. The Honey Puss would stay as long as he could and then leave. She would still be here, somewhere. This is her home, as it is ours.

Turtle,

who brought her babies

I wonder whether Turtle remembers what happened; that is, whether she has what we would call "memory," and whether the event was sufficiently out of the ordinary to be seared into that memory, as it is now seared into mine. I cannot know. I can only remember, myself. And wonder.

Turtle the tortoiseshell kept company with us at the end of that first summer. Could she have been keeping company with the Honey Puss? She left precisely when he left. Or was she keeping to herself, in the wild, or visiting regularly at someone else's door? We didn't know.

It was a full year before she reappeared, walking slowly out of the woods and onto the driveway, then more surely up the two steps and onto the deck. The trust she had once given us was back, too, aroused from some quiet place in her senses. We fed and stroked her, and exclaimed over her. "Pretty pussycat," I had always whispered to her, savoring the orange-gray-tan-black-white of her, the bib of purest white, and the amusing black mask, splotched unevenly with orange and framing a pair of splendid golden eyes.

She was comfortable with us, as if the intervening year had not existed. And soon she trotted off toward what had always been her thicket, a dense tangle of weeds and berry bushes at the far side of the driveway. But as she crossed the driveway, a tiny black kitten ran out of the thicket to meet her. Slowly, timidly, a tiny tan one came out, too. We called our encouragement, and Turtle returned with the babies, showing them in some way that it was all right for them to follow. (In what way, earlier, had she told them to stay?)

How beautiful this trio was—she of mixed shades, they of single colors. Could the Honey Puss be the father? The tan one was his exact likeness in color, but the black one—more aggressive, more curious—was his likeness in spirit. The little ones were even smaller than the Honey Puss had been when he first danced onto our deck. They were perhaps six inches long, with pointed little faces, tiny fuzzy bodies, and straight upright tails. (If they *were* offspring of the Honey Puss, Roy observed, the bushy tail must be recessive.)

Turtle licked the face and body of one of these fluffy babes as it passed her at the steps. The kittens learned steps. And they learned sipping, at a flat dish of warm milk. The black one understood immediately. The tan one took longer. Turtle just watched. Soon she hustled them back to the thicket, again in language we didn't hear or notice. We missed a lot, undoubtedly, but we saw a lot, too, in this intimate verse from the immense saga of birth and growth and renewal.

The next morning we found the two little ones waiting on the steps in the carport. This was the rainy-weather feeding place, known to Turtle from a year ago. She must have shown it to the babies. Was she pregnant, we wondered, and eager to find a good home for these two, before other babies would need her? Why, now, did she bring them here? Or had they come by themselves? And where was she? So protective yesterday, she was nowhere to be seen today.

We watched the two of them tumbling over each other in the carport—prancing, somersaulting, stalking. We watched them drinking. The tan one was lapping at a corner of the plate where no milk stood, the tongue still working although all the milk had settled into the far edge of the plate. Alas, this was the slower of the two. The black one was quicker and bolder, a joy to watch, but our hearts went out to this tan one, who would have the more difficult life.

Our attention wandered, over the next hour or two, and we noticed only that the kittens had gone when we left for a midday meal with my parents. Had Turtle collected them? Or had their curiosity sent them exploring? An October wind was rising; we noticed the noise-level of the woods as we left the house.

We returned in mid-afternoon to find Turtle waiting for us in the driveway. Unusual. She seemed anxious and needing—watching the woods, asking for our comfort. And the babies? Clearly missing. Had they been harmed? Or killed? No, we decided; she was waiting for them to return; she kept looking toward the carport and toward the woods beyond. Leaves were constantly crashing, a hundred false alarms. We were miserable. "When kittens are given away," Roy said, "this is the way the mother acts. Baffled, expectant, concerned. She knows something is missing, but she'll forget soon." I was not comforted. "She *trusted* us with them," I said. (Had she *given* them to us? I couldn't bring myself to ask it aloud.)

We went into the woods several times, each of us, and then several times together, calling to the kittens and calling encouragement to Turtle. We wanted her to follow, or even to lead. But she was distracted, lagging back, uncommunicative. What had she seen? What did she know? She cried out once—once that we heard, that is, because now the wailing wind and falling leaves were able to drown out her voice over the shortest distance.

She was at the far side of the house with us when we heard her cry, and although we went back and forth across the area for fifteen minutes, we found nothing.

Roy and I were now shouting at each other to be heard. With each step we were trampling a season's crop of brittle leaves, and the wind was now strong enough to fling up heaps of leaves on its own. Damp chill had come into the air. It would be a bad night to be out unprotected.

Roy drove to our nearest neighbors down the hill, asking whether they had heard anything unusual. "A lot of barking," Geri said. "What was going on up there?" So that was it. Another neighbor had two large red setters; every few months we heard them near us in the woods, barking, tearing through the brush. "But they'll only tree a cat, they won't hurt it," said Geri. On his way home, Roy stopped at the house of the setters and heard the blunt truth. They do kill cats, said their owner. Not an accommodating man, he nevertheless agreed to keep the dogs inside tonight. Now, late in the afternoon, they were still out.

Farther downhill, Roy made a final stop; perhaps the babies had been pursued this far. It didn't hurt to ask. No, no sight of them, said the farm woman who listened to Roy's description. She volunteered the opinion that in any case, when they're born this late, "they don't winter."

Roy came home, and we tried together to coax some enterprise out of Turtle, who seemed bewildered and restless but not eager to go prowling. Had she given up? Did she know it was hopeless? Or had she forgotten what she was looking for? She trotted around the deck, alert to every cracking and crashing in the woods. We wandered around ourselves, from outside to inside and then outside again, unable to relax. We looked at the trees silhouetted against the pale sky. The light was dying.

"One more try," I pleaded with Roy, and we went out together through the carport. As I stepped outside, one of the red setters bounded up, large and aggressive, his front paws suddenly up against my shoulders, frightening me. I pushed him away, and he ran out onto the deck, frightening Turtle. We yelled him back toward the carport, and beyond it toward his home across the hillside. He was barking energetically. Was his bark really worse than his bite? Ugly premonitions. We made our own menacing gestures and sounds, and rushed after him.

As we dashed around the carport, we saw the tiny black kitten, high in a tree some thirty or forty feet above us and barely visible to us in the draining twilight—still, however, clearly the object of the dog's attention. The dog stood his ground, barking, for the few seconds until we arrived, and then he fled. We couldn't be sure later who had "found" the kitten. Had we seen it in that instant before we knew the dog had? Or had the dog unwittingly brought us to this tiny treed animal? It was at precisely this spot that Turtle had cried out earlier. But the three of us—Turtle, Roy, and I—had found nothing then.

We tried calling to the kitten but couldn't be heard above the wind. "I'll run and get Turtle," I said, and I dashed back to the front of the carport in time to see Turtle trotting briskly down the driveway to her protected patch of weeds and berries. I didn't think she'd come out. What a harrowing day it had been. How many times had she seen this dog today? What dreadful things had happened?

"Come out now, Turtle Sweet-Thing. We found one of your babies. We need you to bring it down. No more dogs. *Do* come out." She rushed out as though she understood the words, and followed me back to where Roy was trying to keep contact with the kitten. I have no explanation for this. Our previous entreaties all day had produced no such purposeful action from Turtle.

But she seemed not to grasp the situation: that the kitten was above her. We tried holding her in our arms, pointing her worried face toward the top of the tree. No sign of comprehension. We tried pointing, ourselves, but Turtle looked impassively at our outstretched arms and no farther.

Now we were watching the night fall. It was getting colder, blowing harder. It might storm. We could only dimly see the silhouette of the kitten against the bare branches, only dimly see the outline of the branches against the moonless sky. With the rising wind, we could no longer hear the tiny meows that had intermittently been sent down to us. It seemed as though Turtle never heard them.

Now we tried a flashlight, shining it mostly on the ground or on the lower part of the tree, hoping not to frighten these animals any further. Shielding the beam, we directed the light at Turtle, then at the kitten, to tell them about each other. Maybe it was foolish—maybe they already knew about each other—but we couldn't be sure.

Then gradually, so gradually, the kitten began to edge down the tree trunk, backwards as was quite correct, holding on with its tiny claws. Down, down, so short a distance at a time. Sometimes a lurching, a scrambling, into the next crotch of branches. Finally a fall—or possibly a jump—for the last fifteen feet. Then it got quickly to its feet and bounced off, with Turtle following, into the nearest undergrowth. We could see its walk in those few steps: the movements of a healthy young creature. Apparently unharmed. Undoubtedly wiser. A survivor!

Yet we never saw that little black one again. Turtle came mooching around the next day, more affectionate and more needing than usual, but placid. She spent a good bit of time with us in those next few days, but the little one was never with her. We speculated that maybe he had "come of age" through this adventure and was no longer tied to her. Maybe he had been injured, after all, and was lying in the brush somewhere—mending, or dying, or already dead. Maybe she had "lost" him again. Or maybe he was back among the weeds and berries, under stricter orders this time.

We never saw the little tan one again, either, and we grieved over the short life of this creature, so young that it hadn't yet learned to lick itself clean; its little bottom had been messy with dark traces of excrement still clinging to the honey-colored fur. We couldn't imagine this tan one surviving an attack from the two setters, so large, quick, strong, experienced, bloodthirsty. Only in our mind's eye did we see the tan one again, and we flinched from the vision and hoped only that the end had been swift. Perhaps the death of the tan one had secured the life of the black one, giving the black one time to escape. Or perhaps it was the other way around; the black one had run free, leaving the tan one, bewildered and slow, to the dogs.

Comfort, of a sort, from Roy: "Animals in the wild don't usually die peacefully of old age. And the law of the wild doesn't have any time-outs, doesn't make any exceptions for the attractive creatures. It may seem cruel, but that's the way it is. It just *is*."

Had I believed, in providing this strange place—not fully wild and not fully protected—that we could get a "time-out" for Turtle and the others? I think so. Revising this idea was hard for me. I spent some time wanting to apologize to Turtle, who had perhaps trusted in our absolute protection. Had we failed her, in offering what we could not guarantee? Or had she failed the babies herself, in some way? We hadn't seen it for ourselves, and even if we had, we might not have understood it properly.

But if the law of the wild has no room for a judgment of cruelty, it also has no room for an accusation of blame. And I came to think that it was no one's "fault," but was one of the endlessly repeated chapters in the lives of these animals. The stronger against the weaker. The quicker against the slower. The larger against the smaller. That's the way it is. The only thing that made it different this time was that we had seen some of it, and had brought the exquisite burdens of human thought and feeling to it.

But what did it mean to Turtle? She was stunned and distracted, one day; calm, the next. How often in her life had she experienced this abrupt termination of her motherhood, this death or disappearance of her babies? She was truly the survivor, though. She would live on with us, more or less faithfully, in this more or less protected place, for quite a few more years. But she would never again bring any kittens around.

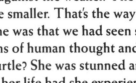

On Reproduction

Reproductive patterns differ between feral and household cats. For one thing, puberty seems to come later for the cat on its own. The Devon farm cats studied by Macdonald and Apps are described in a BBC documentary as "seldom reaching sexual maturity before they are a year old." At that, they may be precocious; Michael Fox, an authority on animal behavior, writes that while female domestic cats reach puberty anywhere from three and a half to nine months of age, "free-ranging females may not reach puberty until fifteen to eighteen months." Males are similarly slow to mature. Bonnie Beaver, in her comprehensive book on the veterinary aspects of cat behavior, concludes that males are generally capable of complete copulations between nine and twelve months. "In the wild, however," adds Beaver, "cats may not reach this degree of maturity until eighteen months of age."

As if to show the contrariness of these cats, the females of Marion Island (2,100 kilometers southeast of South Africa) produce their first litter during the first season following their birth; they reach sexual maturity at approximately eight months, according to Rudi van Aarde. The males of Marion Island are not far behind, attaining full reproductive capacity at ten to fourteen months. Why should the animals on Marion Island (described by van Aarde as "an environment virtually uninfluenced by man") be closer to the pampered pets inside our homes than to the "semi-dependent" farm cats of Devon? "Size is apparently the governing factor," says van Aarde; females begin breeding when they weigh about 2.5 kilograms, and males begin sexual activity when they weigh about 3.5 kilograms.

For many years, it was thought that domestic cats did not breed at all in the wild. A major game survey of the north central states, done by Aldo Leopold in 1931, found only seven dens with kittens—"convincing evidence that breeding in the wild is so rare that it can almost be considered exceptional." Combining the wisdom of sportsmen, naturalists, scientists, officials, and landowners, this survey recorded additional dens under old buildings, but rejected these as lacking evidence that the cats could produce "a truly wild den."

Leopold was supported in his conclusion by a master's student investigating the feral house cat in Oregon's Willamette Valley; in 1940 Nils Nilsson saw no kittens "in areas that might indicate their being born in the wild." Both

Leopold and Nilsson were aided in their conclusion by what they perceived as a scarcity of females. In Leopold's words: "There is a contention almost universal among woodsmen in the north central region that wild housecats are mostly toms. . . . It is possible to assume that the rarity of dens of young in the wild is due to the rarity of wild females." Nilsson had taken 147 cats, 77.5 percent of them male, and he agreed. Ten years later, Earl Hubbs thought the mild climate of the Sacramento Valley might be responsible when he found "numerous" cases of feral cats breeding in the wild, several miles from farm buildings, and when he found the sex ratio "very nearly balanced."

Typically, though, sex ratios have not been balanced. A study on the food habits of feral cats in Oklahoma found 63 percent to be male. A study on the food habits of feral cats in Victoria (Australia) found 68 percent to be male. Thus, when two researchers logged in only 47 percent males among the feral cats in their study of wildlife rabies in Tennessee, they sought to explain the discrepancy: "It is possible that the large males avoided capture by accidentally springing the traps prior to complete entry."

The expectation continues that males will be more numerous. A recent study of feral cats on San Nicolas Island turned up a figure of 61 percent male. "Overall, it does not seem unusual to have more males than females," says the 1981 report, and it cites an authority on vertebrate populations to the effect that most mammals usually produce slightly more males than females.

But when another recent study of feral cats found a sex ratio of 2.5 males to one female, the researcher paused. Writing in 1977 about the predominance of males on Macquarie Island, Jones concludes: "It is not known if this reflects a bias due to the small sample, a behavioral difference between the sexes, or a real ratio resulting from differential mortality." Van Aarde concurs fully in this speculation, especially after participating in a sophisticated statistical analysis of skull measurements on Marion Island (and finding it a highly reliable determinant of sex) and then discovering that the sex ratio among random skulls "did not deviate significantly from the expected 1:1 ratio." Van Aarde suggests that because the females on these islands near the Antarctic Circle spend about 80 percent of their time during the breeding season in their subterranean lairs, they are difficult to capture. The females are surely there. The feral cat population on Marion Island has increased by an extraordinary 23.3 percent *per year*! Five cats were introduced to the island in 1949, and the population was estimated at 2,200 individuals in 1975. Females are very much there, in these wild places.

And there the matter rests, for the present. The sex ratio is a matter of some importance because of its implications for population growth. Leopold could comfortably assume, more than fifty years ago, that "the large number of cats known to roam wild" came almost entirely from "drift"—that is, "from cities, villages, abandoned dwellings." But if feral cats can breed as readily in the wild as domestic cats can breed "at home," then the consequences in terms of population could be disastrous.

Wolski sees no threat of overpopulation among his farm cats in upper New York State. "Kittens are born in the spring and early summer, and are often not weaned until late fall," he writes. "Because they nurse for so long, queens usually only produce one surviving litter per year." Van Aarde reports an average of two litters per year among the cats of Marion Island. And three or more litters per year are not uncommon among the free-ranging cats in high-density urban populations.

Comparing cats with foxes (where only the dominant females breed), David Macdonald notes no similar suppression of pregnancy among cats. "They have kittens, who starve; then they have more. It's extraordinary, but they continue to breed regardless of the food supply. Why? My guess is that they simply treat kittens as a dirt-cheap resource; it costs them little to have them, so they have them. And if they're very lucky they survive." (This comment was published in the BBC *Radio Times*, in an article announcing the documentary on Macdonald's research in Devon. The documentary itself didn't soften these hard realities, but showed kittens dead and dying in close-up shots.)

"There is some indication that social factors may be inhibiting reproduction in some cases," says Jane Dards about the cats in the Portsmouth dockyard, but the evidence is not very clear-cut. The population is curiously stable, she reports, "in spite of a relatively high turnover." The Portsmouth dockyard is altogether unusual: a cat population isolated from the outside since the construction of dockyard walls in 1711 and 1864, a high density of more than three hundred cats per square kilometer, and an industrial habitat unexpectedly generous in food and cover. Is there something unusual in what Dards has observed about the stability of this population?

There is much we don't know about reproduction among feral cats. And it would seem almost unnecessary to add that we don't know the size of the feral population. In California, for instance, the Department of Food and Agriculture thinks the state's feral cat population is "quite high"; in North Carolina, the Wildlife Resources Commission thinks the state's population is "not high at all."

But how could we know? Any estimate can only cover the smallest study area (the total population in the Portsmouth dockyard fluctuates around three hundred). Nilsson, however, estimated the feral population in the rural parts of the Willamette Valley to be 11,710. He was working from the number of farm cats (not difficult to compute, with questionnaires and census figures) and from a 5:40 ratio of feral cats to farm cats. He based this ratio on the distance from farm dwellings of his trapped cats, and on noticeable differences in the trapped cats; the cats he considered feral had thicker coats, a "wild and hunted" look, a defiant spirit, and were "away in an instant" when released.

Any larger guess is bound to be fuzzy at the edges or soft at the center. But I asked anyway. Guy Hodge, research director of the Humane Society of the United States, guesses that there are in excess of ten million unowned domestic cats in this country. (He works from a total cat population of thirty-six million, estimated by others, and he subtracts the twenty-three million to twenty-five million pet cats estimated by the pet-food industry.) *Time* magazine, in its December 1981 cover story, estimates a United States population of fifteen million "public" cats. William George, writing about the "preying cats" of southern Illinois (many of them subsidized), projects his numbers to the rest of the nation and gets eighteen million; these are "reproductively viable populations that, without exaggeration, may be described as teeming." The National Cat Protection Society has an ad in *Cat Fancy* stating that twenty-eight million felines in the United States must "fend for themselves."

I have seen one prediction for the United States (for a year already past) of fifty million "homeless" cats. This seems excessively alarmist, but few people doubt that the numbers are increasing around the world—or are, at the very least, merely stable. One of the calmer reflections is by Paul Rees, who has made an extensive survey of feral cat colonies in Great Britain: "Historical evidence suggests that the feral population is not of recent origin and there is no evidence of a recent increase in numbers." The only noticeable decrease I can find is among the feral cats in Rome. According to Ente Nazionale Protezione Animali, although Italy has more feral cats than owned cats, Rome has always been special: now, with the Tiber polluted, the Roman rats living by the river carry deadly disease to the Roman cats.

Elsewhere, in harsh climates and in harsh circumstances, the feral cat survives—and multiplies. Whether it is true that "Mother Nature seems to keep a good control on their number, and I have learned over the years to accept this way," as I am told by Mary George, the cat lady of Newport Beach, or whether it is true that these numbers are now out of control in many places throughout the world, as we are told by the humane societies, I am not able to say.

Perhaps, as Paul Leyhausen explains, the conditions of life for feral cats are simply too varied for us to decide this question "once and for all, for all populations." So, Leyhausen tells me, some populations are stable; some "maintain themselves only because there are always domestic cats going feral," some are increasing; and some are dwindling. That seems as precise a tally as we can get.

Herbert,

who never figured it out

Good old Herbert. A character out of a Somerset Maugham story, perhaps, from the days when the sun never set on the British Empire— when the British civil servant, for all his appearance of substantiality, led a life of some bewilderment in a place he did not understand and among people who did not love him. Herbert stayed with us for an entire winter and then went back where he came from. When I realize that I do not recall the circumstances of his departure, I know that we did not love him.

But we *liked* him, and possibly that was enough for this undemonstrative fellow. We could imagine him as a human being, drinking a cozy cup of Bovril with a friend, reminiscing matter-of-factly about being gassed in the trenches during the First War. He would not have been a beer drinker; no carousing for Herbert. And he would not have been an elegant man; as a cat he walked stiffly, as if wearing shoes that were several sizes too tight.

He was not beautiful in the way that the Honey Puss and Turtle were beautiful, with their alert faces and their magnificent coloring. No, Herbert had a look of failed dignity—of careful sobriety beyond what was necessary for survival. His coloring was ordinary: a few black patches, a dirty white ground. He lacked the fine ruff, the handsome white bib, of the Honey Puss and Turtle. He had none of the wild, rich-coated beauty of the Maine Coon Cat. He was just a *plain* cat, an alley-variety shorthair. He had lovely yellow eyes, but he didn't have the rest of the face for a catfood calendar. Only from the rear was Herbert truly interesting: just below the tail, two exquisite furry roundnesses—high, tight, velvety. . . . Herbert had a fine pair of balls.

Was it Roy's rival maleness that made Herbert wary of him? Or was it Roy's habitual appearance and disappearance in the dreaded Jeep? Herbert usually gave both of them a wide berth. When the Jeep was on the move, with Roy in it, Herbert would flee ahead of it in the driveway, looking back over his shoulder and muttering. (Turtle was more careful, watching quietly from the edge of the driveway.)

Herbert never saw the MoPed of our friend Bruce, but he would have muttered plentifully if he had. The MoPed was indeed a beast of strange size and sound and odor. Turtle had to walk past it once to join us on the deck, and she kept her eyes on the animal at rest as though she expected it to arise at any moment. With creatures of that size, she may have calculated, you can never be too sure.

I suspect that this is why these feral cats have lived as long as they have; they can never be too sure about anything. I was dressing one morning, looking down from the bedroom at Herbert as he lay on the deck. Suddenly he fled. No backward look. No time for muttering. My belt buckle had rattled noisily. What could he have imagined—a gun being cocked? Had he been that close to hunters? "I think not," said Roy. "It sounded more like dog tags clinking together." I was impressed. "Not so impressive," Roy answered. "I was fooled myself. I thought there was a dog nearby."

I was careful not to make that noise again when Herbert was within earshot. I could have shown him it was only a belt buckle, but another time it might really be a dog. Herbert gave me a fair measure of trust: an enormous compliment. I didn't want this trust to dilute his normal caution. Trust was a luxury for him; it was caution that had served him so well for so long.

A feral cat like Herbert lives in two worlds. This animal who would rub sensuously against my legs and sit luxuriantly on my lap would seem to be "domesticated"—and comfortably so. Yet this is the same animal who would have been tearing at the vitals of some other animal only a short while before. Sometimes we saw it and sometimes we didn't. We heard a large bird slamming against one of our windows and thought no more about it until we saw Herbert gorging himself on the half-eaten remains of a pheasant. Herbert looked up at me, blood still on his jowls, then trotted up to the deck to do a complete "toilette" and jump lightly onto my lap. He enjoyed my lap. And he enjoyed that pheasant.

He didn't have affiliation to spare, and I got most of what little he had. But even though Herbert didn't fondle up to Roy, I suspect they had a certain understanding. "There's a *skunk* on the porch," Roy yelled to me one evening, glancing out of the kitchen door. "But Herbert's there, too," I cried, looking out from upstairs and seeing Herbert crouching tensely on a corner of the deck while the skunk waddled over to the dish of Herbert's leftovers. Herbert deferred to the skunk and maintained a motionless vigil. But he shot a few glances over to Roy, safe behind the kitchen door. Did Herbert want Roy to do something? Roy opened the door a crack and made threatening noises at the skunk. The skunk raised its tail, ready to discharge at the kitchen door. But didn't. Herbert suddenly emerged from his passivity to launch a thundering diatribe, a threatening sermon (at which of the other two?). It was more meowing than we'd ever heard from him. But he didn't move. And Roy made a few more of *his* unusual noises. But he didn't open the door farther. Or close it completely. It was a clear victory for the skunk. The skunk clearly knew it, continuing to eat nonchalantly, and finally waddling down the two steps from the deck and moving off into the dusk. And Herbert and Roy knew it, each of them having had his bluff called. When the skunk finally left, Herbert moved easily around the deck—his territory—and Roy sat down again at the kitchen table—*his* territory. If they could have talked to each other, I think they'd have enjoyed reliving this adventure.

But if Herbert didn't have a compelling relationship with us, he had a lively and complicated one with Turtle. At first he was wary of her, unable to be near her for long. He would suddenly panic and rush off into the weeds under the deck. Soon he became bolder and began virtually shadowing her, staying six feet behind her whenever she approached or left the deck (and probably wherever she went in the woods as well). She would look back at him and hiss, occasionally, but we never saw them fight. Turtle would meander away . . . and Herbert would follow. Sometimes she managed to lose him, in ways that we smiled to imagine, but mostly she was stuck with this stodgy pest, and mostly she seemed annoyed.

She ate with her back to him, the ultimate disdain: no interest and no concern. He ate with at least one eye on her, and if she moved away from her bowl for an instant, he was there in another instant, apparently convinced that her food was far more delectable than his own. She might then move to his bowl (to get away from him?), at which point he would show renewed interest in his original bowl; perhaps it had the most delectable goodies after all. Mealtimes weren't always so frantic, but it was always Herbert who initiated this particular choreography.

We came to call this phenomenon "pussycatting": this practice of becoming interested in something only because someone else was interested in it. Surely this word belongs in the language. What is it but "pussycatting" when a person who has been oblivious to the newspaper all day while it has been lying on the kitchen table suddenly picks up the paper with passionate interest when the spouse sets it aside momentarily to put another log in the wood stove?

There was a large component of "pussycatting" in another routine that Herbert and Turtle played out with some frequency—a game we called "Who's Got the Porch." A typical round of play might begin with Turtle lying on the doormat, and Herbert crouching alongside the porch looking up at her. As she becomes interested in a possible snack in the weeds below, he carefully insinuates himself onto the porch. Then, as she hurtles off the porch into the weeds, he heads straight for the doormat and settles onto it. The end? No. He is soon curious about her thrashing in the weeds, and as he trots to the far end of the porch to look over—and finally to leap over—she climbs the steps of the porch and coolly goes for the doormat. He is faked out again. But he launches another round. He ambles off, leaving her with her precious porch and doormat. Sooner or later she leaves the doormat and porch and meanders down the driveway. Why should she guard something that no one wants? Did Herbert know this all along? He materializes to tag after her. Why should he want something that no one guards? But it isn't about the porch at all. It's just a case of "pussycatting"—perhaps.

Who can know what was really happening between the ever-watchful Herbert and the disdainful Turtle? It was all about territory, surely, and about sex and status and survival, not necessarily in that order and not probably in such neat categories.

Herbert began spraying the carport and deck soon after he arrived, hoping to stake out a territory he could call his own. But this was also Turtle's territory, I thought with some outrage, and while she didn't fight him or chase him, she seemed subdued and bothered by his presence. As well she might be. His was a constant presence, in actuality or in lingering fragrance. He sprayed the Jeep, the side of the house, the deck, the carport. The place stank. We had made Turtle a cardboard house in the carport long before Herbert arrived, and he sprayed that, too, like a house painter in a hurry who will not distinguish between wall and electrical socket but will cover all surfaces equally.

I wasn't happy about the odor of public lavatory that began to hang heavily in the outdoor air. But Herbert was all male, and this was Herbert being true to his inner imperatives. He hadn't learned to be *macho* from the movies.

Herbert was often away for several days at a time, "tomcatting"—that's a verb that *is* in the dictionary. And on one of his reappearances, we saw him limping. Our friend Gail, who knows almost as much about cats as she does about people, thought it might be a dislocated shoulder, or a nasty wound, or even a fakery. Herbert would trot up on three paws, holding the fourth one carefully off the ground. Trouble was, he sometimes approached on all fours, needing (or remembering?) to favor his right front paw only at the last minute. His injury couldn't be all that serious. We tried to find it, but he wasn't willing to be held for an inspection. We'd have to wait a few days and see what happened. Just possibly—and it surprised us that we all thought him capable of it—just possibly, Herbert was a fraud. In another day or two, we saw the wound, healing nicely and requiring no further assistance from us. I was sorry to see the ugly gash—sorry in part, I'm sure, because I was chuckling to think that he had conned us, that he had figured out what a pair of softies we were.

We were thoroughgoing pushovers, and Herbert must have known it. Winter was coming, and since he was settling in anyway, we decided to make him comfortable; we'd make him another cardboard house like Turtle's. Hers was a special creation that had taken shape over the months. His merely duplicated the final design: a smaller box placed within a larger box, the margin between inner and outer boxes stuffed with newspapers, and the whole assembly turned on its side (the top now an open front) to make a homey cubicle with insulated walls and insulated roof.

We placed these little houses high off the ground on top of the woodpile: an easy leap for a cat, an impossible reach for a dog. And for further insulation from the bottom, we stuffed pillowcases (yes, real ones: I had never liked the pattern) with those plastic "peanuts" used for fragile mailings. Having an acorn-hoarding instinct and a large basement, we had a sack of these plastic nuts awaiting new uses. We knotted the end of each pillowcase to itself, making a pair of malleable thermal pillows, large enough for a cat's sleeping body, and able to conserve and give back the cat's own warmth. The cats settled in, pushing these pillows into receptive shapes. They knew a good thing when they saw one.

So here they spent most of their cold winter nights, Turtle and Herbert. We fed them on the porch when the weather was clear and dry. We fed them in the carport when it stormed. And between snowstorms they roamed far afield. Herbert was often gone for several days at a time after his paw healed.

But back he came, all that winter, and we were always here to welcome him. Indeed, when the air was bitter cold in the carport, we sometimes held their bowls up to Turtle and Herbert in their houses, rather than put the bowls on the dirt floor and force these hardy creatures to leave their warm little nests. No matter that our hands and noses and ears were soon painfully chilled. Serves us right for forgetting gloves and woolen hats. It didn't make sense, of course; the cats have marvelous fur coats, thick and heavy, and have survived these Vermont winters as far back as there have been cats and Vermont winters. But when you're a pushover, nothing makes sense. The cats thrived on it, and so did we. We began to announce ourselves well before we opened the door to the carport, when we discovered that the door made a grating noise alarming to the cats, and Roy's favorite announcement was an exultant, "Here comes the Big Pushover!" I was just as big a pushover—merely smaller in size.

Spring came, and the little cardboard houses were used less frequently. Herbert and Turtle were gone more frequently, but whether separately or together, we couldn't be sure. We saw them together in the driveway one

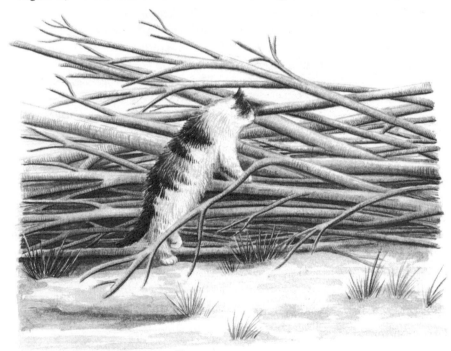

evening, as close to mating as we'd ever seen them. Herbert was definitely interested. Turtle was not. In fact, he had mounted her, but she denied him entry and simply sat there. (We'd never seen her in heat. Was she too old?) Their winter had clearly brought them into a different relationship. There was still a lot of "pussycatting" and following on Herbert's part, but he seemed less frantic. And there was still a lot of territorial outsmarting on Turtle's part, but she seemed more relaxed, less disdainful.

These two were probably not friends, and possibly not mates, but they shared what they had to share—food, territory, us—out of a certain shared practicality. Yet with a certain mutual annoyance. So when Herbert disappeared for good, we weren't surprised. It had been a soft life with us, but not, I think, a comfortable one. He was often perplexed and disgruntled at things we didn't understand, and possibly at things *he* didn't understand.

He was clever, though, in his own strange way, and I marvel at the strangeness of it. He couldn't help but notice the solicitous attention his injury had brought him, and many weeks after the paw had healed, at a time when his life with Turtle was especially vexing and he was seeking some special intervention from Roy, he had trotted up to Roy at a healthy pace, stood before Roy for an instant—and then, in a proven appeal from the past, raised that once-injured front paw! Not so strange. Surely as good a grasp of the proprieties as held by any colonialist among the natives.

On Predation

The image of Herbert cleaning the blood of a pheasant from his jowls will always be memorable to me. The picture of this cat looking up at me from his feast is no different from the picture of a lion on the savannah looking up from its prey into the zoom lens of a distant camera. These animals are cousins. I am not surprised or anguished that a domestic cat should enjoy the taste of the recently living. The wild kingdom is not peaceable. People who are "shocked" at the predatory nature of the domestic cat have learned their zoology from greeting cards.

The cat is a carnivore: an eater of flesh. The cat is a predator (and a skillful one): an animal that preys on other animals. But what precisely does a feral cat eat? And with what effect on the populations being preyed on? Over the years, these questions have stirred dismay and disbelief: that virtually the same puss who graces our hearth would "viciously" devour the still-warm body of some furry little animal, would "cruelly" silence the voice of some lovely songbird. The feral cat, of course, has no such feelings. It eats to live, and it feels no more malice in the acquisition of a meal than we might feel in the purchase of a rib roast from the butcher or a frozen turkey from the supermarket. It is we who bring emotion to this activity of the cat.

Cat haters and bird lovers agree: Cats eat birds. The state ornithologist of Massachusetts wrote an impassioned tract in 1916 (a bulletin on "economic biology") called *The Domestic Cat: Bird Killer, Mouser and Destroyer of Wildlife*. I need hardly cite the main thesis of a work so unsubtly titled, but the estimates of Edward Howe Forbush bear quoting: Farm cats and stray cats can be expected to kill at least 700,000 birds a year in Massachusetts, more than 2.5 million in Illinois, 3.5 million in New York State. (A later document, a student thesis, mistyped Forbush's estimate for Massachusetts as "7000,000" and this crept into still later reports as 7 million! Anything was believable!)

These are not outdated beliefs. According to one current writer on animals, feral cats are "a terrible scourge" where songbirds are concerned. Especially with the recent proliferation of cats, suggests another writer, the ecological impact on wild birds "must be tremendous." Feral cats are said to be "free-loaders," hunting chickens and ducks with impunity. To what extent are these beliefs true?

Forbush had hundreds of sources, with hundreds of observations, but he never looked to the cats. He made no attempt to analyze the food still in their stomachs, "for the obvious reason," he wrote, "that a price offered for such stomachs might result in the destruction of many pet cats." Such detailed analysis of stomach contents would wait at least two decades, as would the detailed analysis of scats: fecal analysis. (All non-flesh parts of prey— feathers, fur, teeth, bones—pass through the cat's digestive system relatively untouched, and can easily be separated from other fecal matter for identification of prey.)

The investigations of almost fifty years have now proven Forbush a partisan of birds and an alarmist about cats:

1936, Wisconsin. The investigation of fifty cat stomachs (incidental to studies of the bobwhite quail) produced "scant evidence" of cats killing strong adult birds. But the researcher cautioned about these fifty cats that there had been few chances of taking "the elusive woods dwellers which are most likely to be feral, and also to have the best access to avian prey."

1940, Oregon. "The most important general conclusion" of a master's thesis: the stomach analyses of eighty feral and rural cats "do not bear out the contention that the domestic cat in the Willamette Valley is a confirmed game bird consumer." Mammals made up 61.8 percent of the stomach contents by volume; birds, 18.9 percent; carrion, 10.7 percent; garbage, 6.3 percent; cereal, 2 percent. Scat analyses verified that the diet was primarily of rodent origin. "Results point to the factor of the availability of food as being the key to the cat's diet," wrote Nilsson.

1941, Oklahoma. The examination of 107 stomachs produced an even lower record of bird consumption: mammals, 55 percent by volume; garbage, 26.5 percent; insects, 12.5 percent; birds, 4 percent; reptiles, 2 percent. "Cats of residential areas and those frequenting roadsides appear to be a greater menace to birds than cats hunting in open fields or woods," wrote Frank McMurry and Charles Sperry. But in any case, the data "do not justify the common belief that every roadside or field-roaming cat is in search of avian food."

1949, Michigan. In his article "Farm Cat as Predator," the head of a wildlife experiment station described exactly that: *one* farm cat and the total prey it brought home over a period of eighteen months—1,628 mammals and sixty-two birds. With restrained triumph, the article suggested that this "positive statistical record," while perhaps not typical, casts doubt on the negative reputation of the domestic cat, "a scapegoat with few to speak up on his behalf."

1951, California. A study of the food habits of the feral house cat of the Sacramento Valley found that mammals were clearly the primary source of food (64.1 percent by volume), although birds were substantially represented (25.2 percent). "The 184 stomachs examined in the study," wrote Hubbs, "actually represented 184 cat meals distributed throughout the year. Forty-one of the meals included pheasant or duck, which means that a vagrant cat will average one game bird about every fifth day."

1957, Missouri. The stomachs of 110 cats killed on highways, away from towns or farm dwellings, showed that the primary foods were "injurious rodents" and that "the house cat's feeding is largely beneficial to man's interests." These hunting house cats were found to feed upon small rodents "more than four times as often as upon rabbit, the second most important food, and nearly nine times as often as upon birds."

These findings represent the major early studies in the United States. On the other side of the world, in New Zealand, a recent study of feral house cats in the Orongorongo Valley finds by scat analysis that mammals account for 93 percent of the food, by weight; birds, 4.5 percent. Nearby, in Australia, Coman and Brunner find a similar balance based on stomach analysis: mammals, 88 percent of the diet, by volume; birds, 5.2 percent. "The common belief that feral cats are serious predators of birds," write Coman and Brunner, "is apparently without basis. Although birds were common in all sampling areas, they were a relatively minor item in the diet. Presumably, other factors such as difficulty of capture are responsible for the low intake of birds."

Indeed, the eminent researcher on cat behavior, Paul Leyhausen, considers the hunting method used by the domestic cat "definitely detrimental to success in bird hunting." The cat waits patiently before springing on its prey, and many is the songbird that simply flies away, unaware of the potential danger, while the cat is still waiting patiently. "Primarily," writes Leyhausen, "all cats hunt both birds and rodents with equal zeal, and many obviously prefer eating birds. But they cannot catch them as easily and for this reason with increasing experience many soon give up hunting birds." (Where the relative absence of rodents concentrates the cats' energies on songbirds, adds Leyhausen, the cats "almost always catch only old, sick or young specimens.")

But when birds are available in large numbers, especially ground-nesting birds, they will be eaten in large numbers. Analyzing prey remains and the contents of 125 cat stomachs, van Aarde has determined that the feral cats on Marion Island feed mainly on nocturnal burrowing petrels. Calculating energy requirements of the cats and caloric content of the seabirds, he has determined that a single cat kills approximately 213 of these birds a year. An estimated 600,000 burrowing prions and other petrels are killed every year by the cats of Marion Island.

On islands with relatively few species of mammalian prey, write Fitzgerald and Karl, feral cats "have had to adjust to unusual foods." The island of Helgoland, off the coast of West Germany, offers only the house mouse and the rabbit as mammalian prey; the cats eat a great number of the island's migrating birds. Seabirds of other islands are similarly vulnerable.

Everything suggests that the diet of the feral cat is endlessly adaptable. Coman and Brunner, examining 128 stomachs of feral cats in Australia, find that cats from the bush areas eat mainly the small indigenous mammals, while cats from the improved and semi-improved areas eat mainly the introduced mammals: rabbits and house mice. "It appears that feral cats are opportunist predators and scavengers and that the level of predation on any one prey type will depend largely on its relative availability."

Where wildlife is varied, the diet is varied. The stomach of *one* Australian feral cat was found to contain three geckoes, two dragon lizards, two large centipedes, one stick insect, two skink lizards, two legless lizards, three grasshoppers, and one hopping mouse. (Sounds more like a selection of hors d'oeuvres than an eight-course banquet.) The Western Australian Museum has identified thirty-two species of mammals found in the stomachs of feral cats.

Variation is seasonal within any geographic area. On Macquarie Island, in the Indian Ocean, when petrels and small rabbits are absent during the winter, there is increased predation upon wekas (these are flightless birds) and scavenging on seals. In the Sacramento Valley, when mammal consumption drops off during summer, birds and insects (and even fish) take up the difference. Writes Hubbs: "This seasonal variability of the cat's diet suggests a constant adjustment to availability of various types of prey and is not necessarily a direct reflection of preference."

The cat's only preference is for staying alive. It will eat what it can and must; it will kill when it can and must. It will also scavenge on dead penguins, skunks—again, whatever is available. A letter from Peter Apps describes his recent research on Dassen Island off the coast of South Africa. "I was able to show that although the cats *ate* a large number of birds, they actually killed very few since most of the birds in their diet were obtained by scavenging on the carcasses of birds which had starved to death. This was important since it determined whether or not the cats were to be regarded as pests."

The discussion thus far has concerned the kinds of prey a feral cat will eat. But what is the effect on the prey? The effect on any individual is clear; the individual mouse dies, the individual sparrow dies, the individual petrel or rabbit or gopher dies. But do enough of them die to cause concern over cat predation? The researcher who first looked at cat stomachs, in 1936, states the issue succinctly. "Preying upon a species is not necessarily synonymous with controlling it," writes Paul Errington, "or even influencing its numbers to any perceptible degree. Predation which merely removes an exposed prey surplus that is naturally doomed anyway is entirely different from predation the weight of which is instrumental in forcing down prey populations or in holding them at given approximate levels."

For the most part, the impact on prey populations is unknown. State agencies responsible for wildlife protection and for fish and game management have no hard facts. These agencies report "little if any threat to wildlife," or they believe the cats "probably aren't working any unusual harm," or they figure the net effect "is probably detrimental," or they guess the cats "can do some pretty widespread damage."

Even when the damage is clear, the culprit may be hard to identify. A wildlife biologist in New York State's Department of Environmental Conservation says that "almost all small carnivores, i.e., mink, skunk, weasels, red foxes, gray foxes, fisher, marten, bobcats, are far more numerous and better equipped to take advantage of birds' nests, carrion and small birds and mammals."

Partridges? Feral cats "can and do take partridge," says the director of wildlife in Vermont's Fish and Game Department, "but everything else in the woods has its eye out for partridge, too."

Pheasants? Studies in the north central United States show the principal predators to be skunks, badgers, squirrels, weasels, crows and raccoons; far down the list is the domestic cat.

Songbirds? "Wildlife authorities insist," says the *Encyclopedia Americana*, "that other birds—jays, for example—kill more birds than do cats."

Poultry? From a pest control specialist in California's Department of Food and Agriculture: "Animal control officials report that feral cats cause depredations to various poultry, i.e., chickens, turkeys, etc., but of the overall depredation from wild animals, this is minor."

McKnight mentions still another culprit: "Chickens, turkeys, ducks, geese, guineas, and even domestic rabbits are sometimes slaughtered in some numbers by felines, though probably not so often as by dogs." Feral dogs are of great concern in many states, because of heavy predation on deer and livestock, and because of documented attacks on people. An article by Roger Caras goes far to suggest that feral dogs and feral cats are similar in ways beyond their common reversion to the wild. Caras combines these animals into "wildlife enemy number two" (singular: one enemy), although most of the charges pertain to feral dogs. According to Caras, the feral dog and cat population (singular: one population), if "very much larger," could provide "the straw that breaks wildlife's back."

Surely feral cats have some clear-cut effect on prey populations, but it is apparently less damaging than one might think. Cats consume large numbers of rabbits and mice, but are "ineffective in controlling population buildup and spread" of rabbits, write Coman and Brunner, and "do little to limit sporadic outbreaks" of mice.

Even when feral cats (along with other predators) take almost every last mouse, as in the California area studied by Oliver Pearson, it is wrong to assume permanent damage. Muriel Beadle, in her encyclopedic book *The Cat*, refers to Pearson's work: "If feral cats can so nearly destroy a wild rodent population, they can do a great deal of harm to other species too." I asked Pearson about this assumption. "Absurd," he said. "Feral cats have been terrorizing my study area for one hundred years and haven't done any noticeable damage yet. They are just continuing what the native bobcats used to do." (His studies concern the complex interaction between predator and prey. The greatest predation on voles occurs when the mouse population is declining, says Pearson, not—as previously thought—when it is increasing. To Pearson this suggests that "through their ill-timed predation" the carnivores are accentuating the fluctuations in the vole population and might even be causing the mouse cycle. But the predators don't *destroy* the prey population; when the mouse population comes back up again in a few years, the carnivores also breed up to high numbers again, Pearson explains.)

Feral cats may do more damage in other situations. In Australia, according to Davies and Prentice, "cats are thought to have caused the extinction of bandicoots and rat-kangaroos." On Marion Island, according to van Aarde, it is "feasible to suggest" that cat predation has caused the decline of certain petrels, because on nearby Prince Edward Island, where there are no feral cats, there is no decline of petrels. But it is hard to measure the precise role of the cats. On Macquarie Island, Jones claims that cat predation "must have played a major part" in the reduction of petrels, although he adds that both rats and wekas are destructive to the eggs and chicks. On nearby Campbell Island, the bird populations have been badly depleted, but feral cats are only one of the factors involved, according to Dilks: "The relative contribution of cats and of Norway rats to the disappearance of burrowing seabirds on Campbell Island is not known."

These situations are difficult to assess. Discussing the decline of many species of New Zealand birds, Fitzgerald and Karl concede that the decline "is often attributed to predation by cats, mustelids, and/or rats, but—as several authors have stressed—many factors may have been operating." Among the factors are "destruction of forest and draining of swamps, modification of habitat by herbivorous mammals, pressure from introduced predators and rodents, competition from introduced birds, and the activities of commercial collectors and sportsmen." Nilsson, too, notes the effect of steadily shrinking cover (with woodlands giving way to cropland, and fences getting tidied up); upland game becomes steadily more available to predators. But suppose that all cats were removed from the Oregon uplands, asks Nilsson. "Would this be followed by a great increase in numbers of upland game? Hardly so, for it is the carrying capacity, food and cover of the land that basically determines the numbers of quail, pheasants, grouse and cottontails to be found."

"In the end," says David Macdonald in the BBC program on his research in Devon, "it is not the cat which limits the numbers of its prey, but the abundance of prey which limits the number of cats, for only with adequate food can the cats live and breed."

This brings up the matter of competition with other predators. On Marion Island, van Aarde finds "considerable overlap" in the prey consumed by cats and skuas (these sea birds are natural predators of burrow-nesting petrels). It is "a classical example of competition for food between a natural predator and an exotic opportunistic predator." The effects of competition can be far-reaching, as van Aarde points out. The skuas actually eat penguin chicks and eggs, primarily, but may increase their predation on penguins with the decline in petrels.

Competition exists between the feral cat and any other creature on whose diet the adaptable cat encroaches. William George suggests that the enormous consumption of rodents by approximately ten million cats in the United States countryside—a consumption conservatively estimated at 5.5 billion rodents per year—is a serious problem to our declining raptor population because hawks and kestrels also feed on rodents.

The small island of San Nicolas offers another intricate situation. Here, the feral cat competes for limited prey and space with the rare island fox. But it was only after the fox crash in 1974 that the feral cats expanded to their present numbers. Why did the fox population fall so drastically in 1974? Because wildlife biologists decided that the fox population was artificially high (the product of artificial food sources: leftovers from the Navy mess hall), and that large numbers of the island fox were diseased or deformed (the product of artificial feeding and of increased contact with members of the same species). A large decrease in the fox population followed the cut-off of artificial feeding. So, while the feral cats did not originally endanger the fox, the cats are now a formidable competitor.

In parts of Australia, the cats fill yet a different niche. Coman and Brunner write: "Whether feral cats have been responsible for the decline in numbers of some native mammals is open to question. The once common *native cat* (*Dasyurus viverrinus*) is now either rare or extinct in most parts of Victoria, and introduced feral cats may be doing little more than filling an ecological niche left vacant by the near disappearance of this indigenous carnivore." The niche is neutral, not caring how it is filled, but the feral cat that fills it is considered "vermin" in Australia. The introduction of bounties on these native cats in the early days of Australian settlement surely helped the native cat to disappear, as it helped the feral cat to thrive.

In England, too (where feral cats may run to more than one million individuals), the cats are a definite presence—"perhaps the most numerous mammalian predators to be seen in the British countryside," writes naturalist

Henry Tegner, "exceeding in numbers such true wild creatures as foxes, badgers and otters, and probably outnumbering the stoat and weasel population." Tegner does not say what this may mean to the foxes, badgers, and otters. (Leyhausen brings to my attention the work of Condé and Schauenberg, at the University of Nancy in France, who find that feral domestic cats are, in Leyhausen's words, "not sufficiently competitive where there is still a healthy population of European Wild Cats around.")

Feral cats, of course, occupy virtually the same food niche as domestic cats, as Olof Liberg points out. In his study area in southern Sweden, the house cats and feral cats eat virtually the same food: primarily rabbits, some rodents, almost no birds. Competition could be high when prey is short, notes Liberg, and "should disfavor feral cats most," since they have no human provisioning to fall back on. In Liberg's view, this could help to explain why his study area had almost no female feral cats; a female bringing food to her kittens would be more vulnerable to this competition than a male hunting only for himself. It is startling to think of domestic and feral cats being in competition with each other, when so much attention is given to the competition between feral cats and other species. But this competition is powerful. Liberg suggests that outside of urban areas (where feral cats are basically scavengers) the feral cat populations seem to occur mainly in areas where there are no house cat populations.

It may bother wildlife "purists," writes McKnight, that the cat—"an exotic"—provides competition to such "native predatory species" as the coyote, the bobcat, the raccoon. It does indeed bother people, whether they are concerned about a rare species like the island fox, or whether they unconsciously draw a line between wild animals (good) and other animals (bad). Since the feral animal is doubly tainted by man—having been domesticated, then having been abandoned or permitted to escape—perhaps inevitably it finds itself on the most-unwanted list.

It isn't easy being a predator, but a bad reputation is not the worst of it. An empty stomach is surely more nagging, more life-threatening. An adult cat will eat 5 percent to 8 percent of its body weight per day (or more, if it is feeding some kittens), and even among these able predators, the success rate is often below a respectable batting average. (Nilsson describes a feral cat waiting near the hole of a grey digger squirrel; in the precise manner of academic treatises, Nilsson tells of hiding behind a rosebush thicket, approximately eighty yards from the cat, and watching through 8 × 30 Zeiss binoculars for two hours and forty-five minutes. No squirrel was caught. In more than two dozen such observations, Nilsson saw only nine captures.)

The cats eat, but they don't always eat well. In every survey of the contents of cat stomachs, some stomachs could not be analyzed; they were empty. Among the feral cats of San Nicolas Island, 22.5 percent showed mottled livers, a sign of inadequate diet.

On top of everything else, the predators are themselves preyed upon. Not by many, in the case of feral cats. Great horned owls, hawks, bobcats, foxes. And, of course, dogs. And people.

It is not the place of our hopes and dreams, this world where one animal kills the next. But it is the world as it is, for the feral cat.

No-Name,

who came to us to die

Had I heard it cry? Or had something else attracted my attention? I was working in the kitchen, and suddenly looked through the glass of the kitchen door to see an all-black cat crouching in the middle of the driveway, barely twenty feet from the house. Odd. These cats never took possession of open territory near the house unless they knew us. This cat was a stranger.

I went outside and approached slowly. The cat didn't move. Its body was oddly humped, as if bunched against the cold, but the November afternoon was mild: one of the last days of an indecisive fall before the deep chill of winter. The animal's posture was odd, the head slung forward and bobbing up and down like the head of a palsied old man. Its eyes were dulled: unhealthy-looking somehow, and half-closed. Its whiskers were sparse.

The cat didn't flinch as I came near. It didn't follow me with its eyes as I circled at a distance of six feet. I felt a flush of fear. A freaky cat. In some primitive way, I was afraid to be near it. I went inside and watched from the kitchen, seeing the cat now get up and walk—no, *try* to walk—limping and collapsing with each step as its rear legs buckled. With a determination moved by who knows what inner urgency, the animal continued its crumpled gait, dragging itself to the edge of the driveway and to the little plywood house we had built for one of the earliest of our cats. The house was never used as a "residence," only as a temporary bad-weather shelter, or as a momentary object of curiosity (Herbert would poke around, go inside, settle down, and come bolting out again). The black cat dragged itself inside now, and then wearily, haltingly, came out again and fell on its side on the ground. It lay stretched out in the sunshine, not moving, breathing slowly. This was a very sick cat.

Was it dying? I debated whether to feed it or not. Wouldn't this only prolong its agony? Why not let the poor thing *die*? Or if I *could* restore it to health—and this seemed a dim possibility—where would it all stop? The woods must be full of animals dying early and difficult deaths. I couldn't imagine going among them, ministering to all of them. Yes, but this one was asking, perhaps. This one had come out of the woods.

I didn't make a decision so much as I succumbed to a kind of reflex, making the habitual gesture by which we seek to cure all ailments— offering the cup of tea, the shot of brandy, the spoonful of broth. I put some fish-pungent catfood into a flat bowl and nudged the bowl along the ground with my foot to a point near the cat's drooping and bobbing head. The cat wouldn't or couldn't eat, didn't seem even to notice the bowl. I could see that its body was not emaciated, was not bruised. I thought then about rabies. At the time, I didn't know that one of the symptoms of rabies is a shift in behavior toward an extreme shyness or aggressiveness. When it isn't furious and biting, a rabid wild animal may appear to be tame. And because various animals in these woods can give and get rabies—skunks, bats, foxes—Turtle had been vaccinated against the disease. "You never know where she'll go, in her travels, or who she'll meet," said the vet.

I thought only briefly about rabies and dismissed the idea out of ignorance. I expected a rabid animal to be fierce, and this poor cat was hardly fierce. I didn't have a name for what might be so dreadfully wrong with it, but I was now sure it was dying. I tossed a pebble noisily onto the gravel behind the cat, and the cat made no sign of recognition: not a flick of an ear, not a twitch of a whisker. Was it deaf—all systems failing—or was it too far gone, in any case, to do anything to protect itself?

And now I knew I ought to kill it. I have never killed anything bigger than a wasp (among insects) or a mouse (among mammals), and this poor cat would need a different sort of killing. It would do a different sort of dying. I experienced a shudder of revulsion, but nagging at its edges was a tiny thrill of fascination, even of attraction.

I would have to shoot it. That much was clear. I had never shot at a living creature, and my mouth was dry. I am familiar enough with firearms, having plinked away at plastic jugs on our open hillside. But hunting was not part of my growing up, and I remain uneasy at the idea of killing a creature— even when I know that the killing is for research, or for proper game management, or for mercy. I understand the policies by which deer, turkey, bear, are "in season," and I agree with these policies. But I am not a hunter myself. Roy does our hunting. And while I badly wanted to leave all of this now to Roy, I couldn't; he was away for a few days. I expected a call from him after five o'clock, and in the meantime I would keep an eye on the situation—an increasingly anxious eye.

Turtle, too, gave the black cat her attention, but she didn't go close enough to sniff it. She must have known better than I that the animal was ill and possibly dangerous. For a single moment I wondered whether this was

Turtle's long-ago baby. The same coloring: totally black. But I have no inkling of whether this possibility occurred to Turtle. I did discover that she was no Florence Nightingale. She trotted down the driveway and disappeared for most of the day. When she returned, she went straight to the deck, making a slight detour around the black cat but otherwise giving it only a single sidelong look.

And I, I kept a worried eye on the poor animal for the rest of the afternoon. I imagined some other beast coming out of the woods and tearing into the cat, dead or alive. I know that such things happen in the woods, and I saw no reason for things to be vastly more "civilized" at the edge of the woods, on the gravel of a driveway and in front of a little plywood house. Or was this territory a kind of sanctuary, and did the black cat come here precisely because other animals wouldn't follow it into the open and attack it?

As if responding to my worry, the cat began another trek—a stumbling, limping, staggering toward the carport. I watched from a distance, outside again, transfixed, the gun in my hand. I had wanted to spare the creature a long and painful death, or an even more ghastly and savage death. But the animal was now *in* the carport, and I was suffocating with guilt over my inability to act. I had imagined shooting the cat, had seen the torn skull, the gore, the oozing remains. And I had not acted. Instead, I had spent those moments wondering whether death isn't often violent. Is it ever *easy*? (Only in fairy tales, and not always in those.) I wondered whether many people died calmly, simply ceasing to breathe, drifting off as peacefully as if watching a butterfly on a summer's day. And in the midst of my reveries, the cat attained the safety of the carport. I did not want to shoot it here, fearing a ricochet from the denser gravel underfoot (and, I admit, being unwilling to clean up the remains from this place, our place). The cat lay motionless now, on the step leading from the carport into the house, the same step where Turtle had deposited her babies on that terrible day two years ago.

Roy called, full of sympathy. He knows I'll never be fully at ease with guns. The next day he'd be home, and he'd do what had to be done. He reminded me of another animal that had found refuge in this carport—a hunting dog, several years ago, left behind because it was old and tired, and almost blind. We had protected the animal until the people from the animal shelter came for it. They'd had no lost-and-found calls for it, and their vet found it hopelessly ill, an abscess in its head. We had sheltered it and fed it, but there was nothing to be done for it. . . . Roy knew I didn't want to kill this cat. But if I watched over it, that would be a service in its own way.

I went outside to watch. The cat was now crouching on the gravel floor of the carport. Had it fallen from the wooden step, or was it still searching for the proper place? It seemed not to be breathing. Half an hour later, when I looked out through the door to the carport, the cat was lying on its side on the gravel. I was quite sure it was no longer breathing. On the wooden step just above the cat, a large blot of moisture was settling into the wood. Moisture from the cat's nose touching the step? At the last, it couldn't hold its head up. Or moisture from its mouth—a death drool? When I looked again, an hour or so later, the moisture had dried into the

step, and the cat was still in the same position. Why did I expect its feet to be sticking up in the air?

And so it died. Was this a slow dying, as these things go? Four or five hours had passed since I first noticed the animal crouching in the driveway. I couldn't help thinking that I should have hastened its dying. But, I finally asked myself, for *its* sake or *mine*?

I felt the need for a solemn commemoration of the death and poured myself a drink. I raised the glass. *"L'Chaim,"* I said aloud, talking to no one in the quiet house. "To life." I will always be moved by this Hebrew toast. "Cheers" is only bubbly and vapid, by comparison. To life, then. To a good life and a quick death.

The next day we wore plastic baggies on our hands and lifted the body into a large green trash bag. Aware of our burden—already rigid in its plastic shroud—we drove it to the dump.

On Danger

No-Name is the only cat I have been afraid of, but I was over-dramatic in thinking, however diffusely, of rabies. The animal could have been dying from any number of conditions and diseases.

What health hazards do feral cats pose to human beings? The answer, as might be expected, is varied. "Feral cats may constitute a significant threat to the health of man and other animals," write Howard Hall and Michael Pelton, following their study of wildlife rabies in Tennessee. But the extent of the threat is not easy to measure. "Uncontrolled cats pose a disease threat," concludes Alan Beck, well known for his research on stray dogs, "but the total impact is not completely clear." And some see little threat. Richard Ott, an internationally known clinician teaching at the College of Veterinary Medicine at Washington State University, tells me: "The feral cat is not much of a health hazard to man. Rabies, for example, in a cat population will be self-limiting."

Rabies, of course, is the first disease that comes to mind, and it stays in the mind. After his extensive study of feral cats in the United Kingdom, Paul Rees concludes that the cats are not a serious health hazard "except in the case of a rabies outbreak."

What is the chance of getting rabies from a feral cat? The disease is as widespread, geographically, as the feral cat itself, occurring almost everywhere except the British Isles, Australia, New Zealand, Sweden, Finland, and mainland Norway. But the situation is as varied as the disease is widespread.

In the United States and in many parts of Europe, rabies occurs overwhelmingly among wild animals, not domestic animals; between 85 percent and 90 percent of all rabies in the United States in recent years is among wild animals, according to the Centers for Disease Control in Atlanta. But the feral cat is betwixt and between: not fully "domestic" and not specifically "wild." It is counted among domestic animals, even though it often lives (unvaccinated) among wild animals. The transmission of rabies from wildlife to domestic animals is a real concern. But the reverse is a real concern, too. "The possibility of transmission between cats and foxes, particularly in the British Isles between cats and urban foxes, is one that deserves serious consideration," writes David Macdonald in his book *Rabies and Wildlife*. Great Britain, of course, has no rabies, and has strict quarantines for imported animals. But pets are occasionally smuggled into the country, and Macdonald sees some risk to wildlife in the nightly contact between cats and foxes in Britain; both populations are high around towns. Cats in the United States have shown a substantial decrease in rabies: from 538 cases in 1953 to 96 cases in 1978, although up again to 156 cases in 1979 with the corresponding increase in rabies among wildlife. Thousands of cats are examined for rabies; the number of specimens found to be positive is extremely small. Macdonald notes that susceptibility to rabies varies enormously among species. Domestic cats are "only moderately susceptible."

Cats currently account for only 3 percent of the total cases of animal rabies in the United States, and 3 percent in Mexico and Canada, too. The full profile in each of these countries is interesting. In Mexico, cats are second highest, after dogs. (Mexico is currently undergoing a serious outbreak of canine rabies, and feline rabies will usually increase along with canine rabies.) In Canada, cats are fifth highest, after foxes, skunks, cattle, and dogs. In the United States, cats are sixth highest, after skunks, bats, raccoons, cattle, and dogs. (Skunks alone account for more than 50 percent of all animal cases in the United States.)

True, people are bitten by cats. But only 3 percent to 10 percent of all animal bites are from cats. And only a miniscule number of these cats are rabid. Going back almost twenty years in the United States, looking at the years 1962 through 1979, only one human death from rabies can be traced to a cat bite, while bat bites (according to Alan Beck, former director of animal affairs for the New York City Health Department) were fatal to ten people during a ten-year period.

In Europe, with relatively few bats, the statistics are different. Foxes are the primary reservoir of rabies in many European countries, and dogs are usually the major source of rabies among humans. But Macdonald suggests that "cats continue to be a problem." In the years 1972 through 1976, cats made up 30 percent of all cases of animal rabies (exceeded only by dogs) in a group of countries including Turkey, Morocco, and Algeria.

Most countries do not have accurate statistics on the loss of human life to rabies, asserts Macdonald, "but it has been suggested that there are fifteen thousand deaths in the world each year caused by rabies; some authorities estimate ten thousand deaths for India alone." A total of only 15 human cases was confirmed in Europe during the years 1977 through 1979, according to Graeme Nicholson of the British Veterinary Service, although broadening this area to the "European region" during the years 1972 through 1976, we see as many confirmed human cases as 200 for the Soviet Union and 230 for Turkey. In the United States, in contrast to many other parts of the world, we see only five human cases for the most recent year in which figures are available (1979), and none of these cases is traced to a cat.

What of other diseases? Toxoplasmosis, a parasitical infection, occurs in up to a third of the human population in some areas of the United States, according to the Centers for Disease Control. There are three major sources of the infection, according to the CDC: "The most significant is the transplacental transmission from a pregnant woman to her fetus. Infection can also be contracted by eating raw or poorly cooked meat, most often pork or lamb. Recently we have become aware that oöcysts excreted by cats in their stools can also infect humans." For most adults, the illness is not serious. For congenitally infected infants, though, the disease can cause severe neurologic disorders, mental retardation, and blindness. "Many aspects of toxoplasmosis are poorly understood at the present time," says the CDC, but it reports two to six primary maternal infections per one thousand pregnancies in the United States each year.

On toxoplasmosis, too, opinions differ. Richard Ott writes, "Feral cats are far enough away from human contact so that the spread of internal parasites and toxoplasmosis does not usually produce a human health hazard." But a recent article in the *Canadian Veterinary Journal* spells out quite clearly the routes by which the oöcysts can be dispersed and the disease transmitted to humans (and to vertebrates eaten by humans). Feral cats would seem to play a definite role in the cycle, although it is possible, as reported by one researcher, that "most cats shed oöcysts only once in their lifetime." The connection between cats and toxoplasmosis and humans is drawing continued attention. A doctoral student in public health at Johns Hopkins University has been looking at free-ranging cats in Baltimore, trying to measure the contribution of these animals to the incidence of the disease among humans in an urban situation. His research is still in process.

Plague is another disease with a cat connection. The Centers for Disease Control recently reported two cases of human plague caused by domestic cats; one case resulted in the death of the person. Cats often catch the disease, says the CDC, but rarely pass it on to humans. Previous to this double incident in 1981, only six cases of human plague associated with domestic cats had ever been reported.

The 1980 symposium on The Ecology and Control of Feral Cats included a comprehensive discussion of the health hazards presented by feral cats. Major Norman Southam of Britain's Department of Health and Social Security calls it common knowledge that many hospital grounds have a problem with "infestation" of feral cats. He discusses five human diseases relevant to non-tropical climates, questioning whether any of the diseases provides adequate justification for the entire removal of cats from hospital areas. Rabies? He sees no justification for the wholesale destruction of a feral cat population, unless similar measures are carried out among other forms of wildlife. Toxocariasis? He places more blame on the dog in this relatively rare disease. Toxoplasmosis? Domesticated cats are probably more implicated than feral cats. Cat-scratch fever? A feral cat will turn and run rather than attack a human intruder. Salmonellosis? Other pests, particularly birds, might be more readily incriminated. Southam sums up by saying that the secondary infestations of fleas (with their "much greater psychological, emotional and economic impact") provide more justification for removing cats than the primary infestations of the cats themselves.

Turning from particular diseases to *health hazards*, Southam examines the word "health" as the World Health Organization defines it: "a state of mental, physical and social well-being and not merely the absence of disease." Here, Southam suggests, the presence of feral cats "could conceivably constitute a health hazard under the first part of this definition." The true reasons for wanting feral cats removed from hospital grounds, says Southam, are aesthetic; people find the cats offensive or consider them a nuisance. "Of course feral cats can transmit disease," he concludes, "but the sequence of events necessary for this to occur makes the possibility remote."

If feral cats are not significantly dangerous to human beings, in terms of disease, these animals are quite dangerous to each other. "Among themselves, they have a great disease problem," says our vet, George Glanzberg, and no one can disagree. The highly contagious viral disease panleukopenia (feline distemper), for instance, which is preventable and treatable among house cats, is lethal in a feral population. Unvaccinated and untended, feral cats are at the mercy of each other's diseases. And to the extent that feral cats are in close contact with household cats, the viruses and parasites of the feral animals are soon shared with the domestic animals.

Beyond disease, are feral cats a danger to household cats? Some people think so. In an everyday tone of voice, the woman at our nearby animal shelter tells of a cat from the woods attacking an owned cat and having to be shot. A writer in *Cats Magazine* states that feral cats routinely "prey on household pets." But a neighbor of ours who says he has "a cat and a half" (one in the barn and one in the house) says they get along very well together; the two animals walk along the path together, and at the point where the path branches off toward the door of the house, the house cat continues toward the house alone. And the editor of *Animaldom*, published by the Pennsylvania SPCA, states that "feral cats are not a threat to human beings or domestic pets."

The belief persists that feral cats are dangerous to human beings—that because the cat is an adaptable predator, willing and able to kill various kinds of animal life, it must be an all-purpose murderer, eager to kill all forms of animal life. The suspense novel *Feral*, written by Berton Rouché, deals a deadly blow to the feral cat. Rouché's nonfiction (about perplexing medical puzzles) contains the most detailed of facts and lends a color of reasonable-ness to this thriller about feral cats. But the thriller goes beyond what is reasonable, suggesting as it does that a cat away from the hearth is "evil" and "crazy," with "something odd about its gaze," and is a menace to all living things. Roueché's cats travel in a terrifying mob that fairly quivers with a lust for vengeance; the cats do terrible mortal damage to creatures of all sorts—to birds (of course), to a baby rabbit, a deer, a dog, and finally to a man, two men, more. Where will it end? Where it must end: with the destruction of the cats by a posse of armed men who, in their frenzy, have themselves lost all reason. Here is Our Hero, in his moment of decisive action: "It was frighten-ing, and suddenly enraging. I aimed and fired. I reloaded and aimed and fired again. I pushed in another cartridge. I fired without thinking. I fired without aiming. I fired without knowing what or even where I hit. I heard myself shouting. I shouted louder, and fired and fired and fired." To Roueché, the man with a gun is as crazed and murderous as the cat gone feral—unfair, I think, to both man and beast.

Could a group of feral cats "evolve" (Roueché's term) into a ferocious band of vengeful killers? "It isn't typical cat behavior," says our vet; "you could accuse dogs of that, but not cats." The director of wildlife of the Vermont Fish and Game Department, agrees: "It's not likely. They're so shy, so timid." The executive director of the Elsa Wild Animal Appeal tells me, "The idea of feral animals banding together to 'get' humans is a bit much!" And the noted ethologist Paul Leyhausen, whose cat studies are broad and deep, comments, "Utter nonsense."

I asked Roueché about the premise of the book. Could it happen? Had it ever happened? His reply: *"Feral* could conceivably happen: summer people and others do discard pet cats on the way back to the city, and those cats do multiply and survive. I exaggerated this possibility for dramatic (and moral) effect. It has never, to my knowledge, happened." (There is room for debate as to whether he has exaggerated a possibility or fabricated a fable.) For further information, Roueché suggested that I contact his friend Roger Caras, who liked *Feral.* The reply from Caras: "No, I do not think feral cats ever act as Berton Roueché's cats did in *Feral.* That was a wild flight of fancy only. Feral cats are scared out of their wits of people and spend their life ducking the terrors of man and dogs." In his own book, *Dangerous to Man,* Caras says that few of the lesser cats (and carnivores in general) "ever really are dangerous to man unless cornered, captured, or otherwise molested." According to Caras's book, "It is a rare carnivore that doesn't give man a wide berth."

Feral cats are *wild* (relatively wild or completely wild), but this is quite different from being man-killers. "I don't think there is another animal in the Vermont woodlands that is as 'wild' as a domestic cat reverted to the wild," says a staff member of Vermont's Agency of Environmental Conservation; "one would want to be very careful on a chance encounter, especially if such a cat were to be handled for any reason." There is no disagreement on this. "Domestic cats gone wild often become as wild as true wildcats," writes Mike Tomkies in his book on Scottish wildcats. "And the longer a cat lives in the wild, the wilder it becomes," says Tom McKnight. He reports a half dozen cases of feral cats "unhesitatingly attacking humans who bothered them." (These provoked attacks seem entirely reasonable to me!)

I can find no evidence whatsoever that the feral cat is a man-killer. On the other hand, man is a cat-killer. I am told by the wildlife agencies in many states that some landowners and hunters simply "eradicate" any feral cats they see, because of real or imagined destruction of poultry and game birds. "Game wardens annually trap or shoot thousands of wild domestic cats," states *Collier's Encyclopedia*. Humane organizations trap and "euthanize" thousands more.

There is danger where feral cats are concerned, but people are far more dangerous to feral cats than feral cats are to people.

Sylvester,

who couldn't stay

He was exuberant and pushy, and if he had spoken our language, he would have spluttered. But he spoke his own language, in a high-pitched squeak full of passion. Even silent, he had a palpable life force, his keen face alert and intelligent. He was mostly black, with bib and whiskers of brilliant white. He was messy and wild, and we called him Sylvester.

Echoes, perhaps, of the cartoon cat Sylvester. We saw him regularly on TV in a catfood commercial. Or echoes of *Felis silvestris,* the species complex that includes the European wildcat (F. silvestris silvestris) and the African wildcat (*F. silvestris lybica*). It is from the African wildcat that the domestic cat is most likely descended.

Even the great naturalists have named their cats with a certain whimsy, a certain childlike certainty. Mike Tomkies, who wrote of his Scottish wildcats, had a Sylvesturr; I am afraid he also had a pair of kits called Cleo and Patra. The great Konrad Lorenz wrote of his house cats Thomas I and Thomas II (and *his* wife Pussy). And Paul Leyhausen, the giant in research on cat behavior, had a string of mostly unnamed cats (M3, M12, W5, etc.), along with a very nice animal called Herbert. With these examples, I don't need to apologize for the names we have given our feral cats. I smile when I say, "We named her Turtle because she's a tortoiseshell." It was more complicated than that, and I thought of changing her name when I grew very fond of her. But once it was Turtle it could never be anything else.

All our cats have had additional names. Not the way T. S. Eliot saw it: first the "sensible everyday" name, then the special name peculiar to the particular cat, and finally the name only the cat knows—and ponders raptly for hours on end. No, our cats have always had several names, but one name has been a description and not a name: a description we use with ourselves, and not a name we use with the cat. The Honey Puss became His Roundness, and Turtle became Little Miss Meatloaf. I am sorry to say that Herbert, at least to Roy, became the Dim Bulb. (I have already explained that these two had an intricate relationship not wholly rewarding to either of them.) And with Sylvester's black hair, long and wild, he became the Dust Mop. These names were endearments, in their way.

That's just the beginning for a feral cat—who can pick up a name as easily as it can pick up and move, and as often. I saw a black-and-white cat, only recently, in an open field about a mile down our dirt road. (The place was near the house of a newspaperman who, coincidentally, had once written sympathetically about stray cats.) I have no doubt that this was Herbert, good old Herbert, although it is hardly possible that he was still "Herbert." He might be Tobias or Sam or Old Lardy, or who knows? He almost certainly would not be Herbert. No matter. A cat by any other name can live as well. He looked "at home" and in fine shape. Good old Herbert.

But when Sylvester arrived on our deck, he was probably too young to have had other names. He came out of the woods, this sylvan creature, giving us another not-quite-conscious reason for calling him Sylvester.

I was in the Midwest, giving some lectures, when Roy first noticed "a black one" hanging around, looking for a hand-out. We were struck by the intensity of this beautiful animal, and wanted to feed him at least partly to be able to keep looking at him. But he came only when Turtle wasn't here, and we thought he should be fed only when she *was* here; she shouldn't think she'd been supplanted. Soon enough, he came when she was eating, and I fixed another bowl for him. Our cat psychology was on shaky ground, though; the cats knew better what was happening. With Sylvester so near, Turtle could not eat. She watched him closely, her tail flicking back and forth, her body a firmly shaped meatloaf. Sylvester ate furiously, and when he had finished his food, he moved toward hers. At this, she advanced on him ever so slightly and raised a warning paw. She swiped at the six feet of air between them. Sylvester fled. She seemed to have the situation in hand.

Again, how little we knew. We started out for a walk together, Roy and I, late that afternoon. It was unusual for us to go walking at that hour, but it was a fine fall day, one of the last mild days of autumn. Turtle followed us all the way down the driveway and this, too, was unusual. She called to us then, plaintive little meows, until we were almost to the next driveway, a tenth of a mile down the road. We couldn't go farther. We turned back and had just reached her—the three of us on the same side of the road—when a car approached. At the last possible instant, she decided to cross to the other side of the road. She dashed across, and the front wheel on the far side of the car missed her by no more than twelve inches. We gasped. How often does she do something like this? By then, we guessed she was terribly apprehensive. Poor worried Turtle. We all walked slowly up the driveway, Roy and I talking to her in extravagant tones, and Turtle taking her time now that she had us back again. She stopped to sit in the driveway, and she stayed there until we rounded the bend near the house and couldn't be seen any longer. Then she walked slowly to the house herself, to sit in the sun on the deck. Roy commented on how old she seemed, her legs so bowed out, her walk so heavy. The black one, aggressive and eager, would be a handful.

Sylvester returned, of course. And we fed him, of course. Partly because he had us hooked; we didn't know how to say no. And partly because we had him "trained"—or so we thought. He would invariably go to her bowl when he had finished his own (or before), but Roy would be standing between the advancing Sylvester and the defending Turtle, and a slight movement from Roy would give Sylvester second thoughts.

How different they were. Turtle was calm, minding her own business, all *round.* Sylvester was rambunctious, meddlesome, all *ragged.* She was primarily tidy, as we came to think of it, doing her toilette soon after each meal and never spilling her food. He was secondarily tidy, dropping great wads of food onto the ground or deck and then going back for them after the dish was taken away. He always ate energetically, running from one side of the plate to the other—even when it was milk! He did his toilette only after he was sure there was nothing more to eat.

Roy loved the things about Turtle that reminded him of me; he saw her as solemn and tidy and unruffled. And I loved the things about Sylvester that reminded me of Roy; I saw Sylvester as messy and lively and enthusiastic. The cats returned our special affections in special ways. Turtle drooled when Roy petted her, but didn't do this with me. Sylvester licked my hand when I petted him, but didn't do this with Roy. Was it something about males and females?

Everything seemed amicable enough between them, but we saw her reach out once, almost absentmindedly, and dab him on the head with her paw. He cringed and cowered, and moved out of range. He hadn't been bothering her, unless his very presence was an intrusion.

We didn't know where these two spent their time when they weren't with us. They were on or near the deck several hours a day, getting food and attention, napping. What they did with the rest of their time, and whether they did it together or separately, were not for us to see.

Until the first heavy snow of the year. We already knew, from the paw prints, that Turtle sought protection in the carport with every sprinkling of snow. But as a foot of snow built up in this storm, and Turtle took her meals in the carport (served through the mudroom), Sylvester joined her here. "Wherever Sylvster *really* lives, he's living here tonight," said Roy, admiring the good sense of the animal. We wondered what Turtle thought.

Over the next week or so, Turtle spent a lot of time in her cardboard box on the woodpile. Sylvester spent a lot of time on *top* of her cardboard box. This involved some unsettling of logs and some jostling of Turtle, but if she was annoyed, she wasn't sufficiently annoyed to leave the box. We tried to get Sylvester interested in a second box, newly outfitted; he sniffed it and backed off. Then Turtle got interested in the new box. She walked into it, sat down, tucked her elbows under her, and stayed. The two of them soon worked it out, not in a way that made sense to me, but I concede my imperfect understanding of these matters. Turtle went back to her original box, and the new box remained empty. And what of Sylvester? He took a position atop the woodpile, midway between Turtle and the door to the mudroom. That must have seemed like a good spot.

"Let's go check the livestock," Roy would say, leaving the warmth of the house to visit our two wild visitors. Turtle would yawn and stretch inside her cardboard box and jump down to greet us (or wait there to be greeted). Sylvester would skitter down the logs to dance excitedly around us. They were having a reasonably good time of it together in the carport. We often saw one of them approach the other, sniff the other's nose. They seemed comfortable with each other, and the winter continued.

It wasn't only Turtle and Sylvester that winter. There was a second black cat, for a day, more audible than visible. We heard a threatening growl at the turn of the driveway, and saw the newcomer and Sylvester face each other off. That night a howling woke us, and Roy switched on a light to see the intruder tearing down the driveway. We found tufts of black fur—we don't know whose—down by the mailbox the next day. (Is this what it means for the fur to fly?)

Is it significant that we saw Sylvester mounting Turtle on the morning after his "rival" was routed? Turtle—all round—sat on the snow in the driveway, Sylvester straddling her but apparently not penetrating her. (Her rump was down, and her tail was wrapped around her.) She seemed to accept his presence, but after his thrusting stopped and they moved apart, he flinched at her every move. She was not aggressive toward him; she was simply not interested in him.

And now Sylvester followed her *everywhere*, coming within a few feet of her, sitting when she sat, watching her constantly. Whenever one of us went down the driveway for the mail, the two of them would trot along behind, and when we turned back to the house with the mail, they would sit in the driveway together. Were they companions, then? For much of the day they seemed to be together: under the deck, in the carport, on the driveway, in the winter-dry weeds. When she needed to defecate, once, she jumped down from the deck, found a place nearby, did what she had to do, and covered the droppings with snow. Sylvester jumped down from the deck and did the same—at a spot not three feet from hers.

Suddenly, she had this copycat thoroughly intimidated. She could stop him with a look. She didn't even need to raise a paw. We were impressed and mystified by this turn of events. What had given her the upper hand? Had they fought? Were they courting? Were they waiting for yet another change in the relationship? They were still companions. On the first springlike day, they basked together in the sunshine on the deck like a pair of tired clerks on their first day at the seashore, their faces to the sun, their eyes closed, their bodies sprawling.

Then Sylvester disappeared for more than a week. When he returned, one evening, Turtle saw him slowly approaching and moved off into her thicket on the far side of the driveway. I was startled myself at the sight of Sylvester. He was pitifully thin—no, it was hair loss, exposing a blotchy skin on both sides of his body. I didn't want to touch him, but he was wary of me anyway, ready to run off at any sudden move of mine. I put a good portion of food outside for him, and he ate steadily, listlessly. He settled onto a corner of the deck in the growing darkness.

I checked a book on cat care. Was it mange? Was it something contagious? I was concerned about Turtle. It was apparent, though, that she wouldn't visit while he was here. And he was still on the porch as the spring night closed in.

We'd have to get him examined. What a struggle that would be. Sylvester had almost certainly never been inside a dwelling, probably never been extensively handled. Were we now going to get him into a cat carrier, drive him to the vet, have him poked and probed, get him back into the cat carrier? It seemed enormously difficult. But what were the alternatives? We could stop feeding him and hope that he'd stay away from here (and away from Turtle). Or we could "do away" with him (I couldn't bring myself to say "kill" him). Roy said he could more easily shoot Sylvester than deny him food.

We studied our other cat books. The hair loss might be caused by eczema—from loneliness, or from competition with another cat! Or it might be caused by ringworm and be transmittable to us. Or it might be caused by fleas and be hard to cure.

I expected to feel guilty at the thought of killing Sylvester, but I only felt sad. I expected to feel appalled at playing God, but Roy thought we were playing God, whatever our actions. Even a lack of intervention is a kind of intervention, when a decision is involved. We'd see the vet and take it from there.

Roy got Sylvester easily into the cat carrier and closed the lid. During the short trip to the vet, Sylvester cried a lot and clawed frantically a few times, but mostly lay still. He had urinated, and the liquid was sloshing back and forth on the bottom of the cat carrier. Roy imagined that Sylvester was furious; I imagined that he was frightened.

Our vet was now a man with a warm voice and good hands, and Sylvester allowed himself to be handled. "It's not contagious," the vet began. "But his skin is thinning. It's probably a hormonal problem: maybe adrenal, maybe thyroid. If that's what it is, he was born with a tendency toward it." We could find out for sure, the vet explained, but it would be expensive and complicated, and in any case it would be impossible to give daily medicine to an animal living in the wild. "Take him home. Nature sometimes has some surprising cures. In time, though, his metabolism might be affected severely." Too bluntly, I asked, "Should we kill him if he seems to be failing?" The answer was no help to me: "Not if all he has is a cold for a week."

As we left, the vet said, "This is a nice animal." I found myself saying how unbelievably interesting Turtle is, and he replied, "But this one's nice in his *own* way."

At home, Roy opened the cat carrier on the deck, and Sylvester stepped out and walked slowly toward the bend in the driveway. His tail was matted with urine. He had a lot of washing to do.

Soon he was back on the porch, crowding Turtle, jealous of the slightest attention to her. Why did I want this rambunctious fellow? I had forgotten to ask how long it might take before we'd see whether he was getting better or worse.

It took exactly two weeks to see that he was suddenly more aggressive, swatting at Turtle, lying nearest to the kitchen door, marking out the whole deck as his territory. She chose to avoid the situation by avoiding him. She ate hastily and departed, disappearing for long hours down the driveway.

"She's going to need us more and more, as she gets older," said Roy, "and we can't let him push her out—and that's what he *will* do, more and more."

"But I can't turn him away like some waif out of Dickens," I said.

"It isn't easy for me, either," said Roy. "He's a surrogate son to me, too. But I shouldn't have let you anthropomorphize him. He can take care of himself very well. He did, before he came to us, and he's much bigger now—much stronger than when we took him to the vet."

We talked about it for days. "It won't be easy for me, but I can take him about ten miles away," said Roy. "I don't want to hurt him, but I don't want *him* to hurt *her.* And there's no halfway; he'll take over, because of his life force. But because of his life force, he'll be okay away from us. He has to go."

Roy may not have convinced himself, though. He shouted and snarled at Sylvester a few times over the next few days and was glad to see Sylvester intimidated. "Maybe he knows I'm going to take him away if he comes back," said Roy. But then Sylvester did come back, more intrusive than ever. Turtle began to mutter in complaint, yet she didn't raise a paw to him, and her glance had no effect on him. She didn't stay long whenever she appeared. Sylvester had claimed the place. "It's his way," said Roy. "He has to do this. And I have to take him away." We had chosen to protect Turtle, even though she wasn't asking for protection.

She hardly gave Sylvester another look, as Roy took him off in the car, in the cat carrier. And Sylvester hardly gave Roy a backward look as he moved off into the woods when Roy released him. "It was as if he lived there," said Roy. "And he does," he added softly. The place is near a stream, Roy explained to me, so he'll have plenty of water. And it's near a road with several houses on it. And it's summertime, with a lot of little critters to eat. "He'll be just fine," said Roy, ". . . if he beats that hormonal problem."

I have often wondered whether we could have handled this some other way. It would have been absurd to kill Sylvester in order to save him from death. But I was uneasy about having given to him, and then having stopped, when it was no fault of the recipient that things had changed.

In a corner of my mind, back among the truths that are difficult to know, difficult to speak, is the shadow of a thought that we were protecting Turtle from a possibly living Sylvester, yes; but we were protecting ourselves, too, from a possibly dying Sylvester. He would die, as do all living things, but we wouldn't have to see it.

Sometimes all choices are difficult; comfort is not to be found. We had been preoccupied by the decision about Sylvester for days beforehand, and for days afterward we simultaneously hoped and feared he would return. But Turtle—living only in the present—had no such concerns. She knew only that she had us to herself now, and that was enough. She claimed the deck and gave herself over to excessive bursts of purring, interrupting these vibrations of contentment with an occasional sigh of purest pleasure.

On "Togetherness"

No one knows what enables a cat to form close and lasting bonds with people. Leyhausen's theory in his book *Cat Behavior* is that for an adult cat, "the social sector is fully occupied with guarding territory, defense, rivalry, and mating," and there is no chance for the cat to express its "residue of propensities for juvenile activities." Since a human being "doesn't elicit defense and/or attack as uncompromisingly as an adult cat almost always does," the cat's juvenile propensities can be released, or even revived, by any person who has "a little skill and the necessary sympathetic understanding." This would explain why we see the same kind of behavior between a cat and its humans as we see between a kitten and its mother. "The hypothesis is supported," Leyhausen adds, "by the fact that in sexual behavior, which of course necessitates temporary contact between the partners, juvenile activities also play a certain part."

But what kinds of social bonds do cats have with other cats? Beyond the brief upbringing, the brief courtships and matings, is the cat a solitary creature? Until recently, the answer was unequivocally yes. In 1969, for instance, a book on the behavior of domestic animals could discuss every possible category of domestic cat behavior—ingestive behavior, sexual behavior, maternal behavior, learning behavior—but not social behavior. Presumably, it didn't exist. In 1973 a scholarly article comparing the social systems of various animals could identify the lion as "the only truly social felid." In 1978 a veterinarian's guide to domestic cats could state that "one of the reasons cats make such good pets is that they are not social."

But, in Leyhausen's words, "the only mammal one could conceivably speak of as being socially indifferent is a dead one." His essay in 1965 on the communal organization of solitary mammals (with special attention to free-ranging domestic cats) was enormously important. "As far as I know," he wrote, "the existence of a social pattern into which individual, solitary lives might be woven has never seriously been considered. The basis for any such pattern could be found in territorial behavior."

Leyhausen posed such a pattern for the free-ranging domestic cat, with territories that are not exclusive to each cat, but are noted very closely by each cat. Scent-marking does not intimidate other cats, or inhibit them from traveling the same route, Leyhausen observed, and he suggested as "pure speculation" that scent-marking must have "at least one other function if not more"—perhaps "to avoid unexpected encounters and sudden clashes," and perhaps "to tell who is ahead on the road and how far, and whether he can be met if required." Whatever the precise function of scent-marking, and of the various visual means of communication noted in certain free-living domestic cats (making scratch marks, leaving feces exposed), the very existence of this kind of territorial system indicates a close mutual awareness among cats.

This system may tell us more about what keeps cats apart than what draws them together. Perhaps, as Bonnie Beaver has observed, "Most cats form a much stronger bond with home range and territory than with any social being." Perhaps, for the cat, the solitary life is all. Certainly the domestic cat has developed nothing like the cooperative hunt of the lion. On the contrary, the cat is very good at stalking and killing its prey by itself. (The size of the prey confirms the arrangement; there's not enough meat on the average vole to be shared. The domestic cat had best be a lonely hunter.)

However, as Leyhausen hypothesized in 1965, "mammals that normally live solitary lives often seem to have a faculty for changing to some form of group life." In fact, one argument I have encountered in favor of a more social life for the cat is the existence of the sixteen distinct body and tail postures and the nine distinct facial expressions (all documented, incidentally, by Leyhausen) that are available to the cat when it meets its own kind.

Only recently has the social behavior of the free-living domestic cat been thought worthy of methodical investigation. Leyhausen's remarkable studies were very methodical, but were done mostly on caged animals, with supplementary observations on free-ranging domestic cats and on various animals in zoos.

To my knowledge, the first quantitative study of free-ranging domestic cats was John Laundré's investigation in 1974–1975 of ten Wisconsin farm cats. "The cats' social order was poorly formed," observed Laundré. "Little group bonding behavior was noted; the social order was not well established below the dominant individuals, and it seemed most intense only during congregation." (The cats assembled twice a day at milking time for a handout.) Laundré assumed that these cats "formed a group to utilize a specific food source," and he observed that "the solitary life-style was still available"—used daily for its advantages in hunting. The cats thus fluctuated "between both life-styles" and, in Laundré's conclusion, "never would fully develop the refined intricacies of social or solitary living because they never fully depended on either for survival."

Recent observations have more firmly favored the social over the solitary. Here is David Macdonald, describing his small colony of farm cats in rural Devon: "There has been a tendency to categorize cats as solitary carnivores and to dismiss groups of farm cats as unstructured aggregations around the milk churn. This was not born out by our observations, which suggested that the colony had a complex social structure." Here is Macdonald, this time in a BBC documentary, describing the work of Jane Dards at Portsmouth dockyard: "Her observations support the growing belief that the cat is indeed a social animal—at least when faced with ample food and shelter." And from Roger Tabor, describing his research on the behavior of feral cats in London: "My recent work certainly seems to be confirming the suggestions made first in the 1950s by Paul Leyhausen that apparently solitary animals might have a greater degree of social life than was then believed." And, from Tom Wolski, too, describing his farm cats in New York State: "I'm dealing with a social animal—they are *highly* social, in their long-term relationships with each other, their continuing contact with each other."

But, as always, the free-ranging cat has many lives. Comparing the social organization of domestic cats in two different environments in Scotland, L. K. Corbett finds that the farm cats of North Uist Island live a communal life, while the feral cats on the uninhabited Monach Islands live a solitary life. The farm cats have overlapping home ranges; the feral cats have exclusive territories. The dominant feral cats do not bury their feces (which, according to Corbett, "may act as visual/scent posts reinforcing the presence of the territory holder"); the farm cats and subordinate feral cats usually do bury their feces. Rabbit is the basic food for all these cats. But when rabbits are in short supply, the farm cats also have the possibility of mice, hand-outs, and scavenging around the farm. The ability of the farm cats to exploit these alternatives, suggests Corbett, "is reflected in their flexible social organization." Among the feral cats, on the other hand, competition for the winter-scarce rabbits "may have led to a system of exclusive territories."

Because different social behavior is produced by different circumstances, and because the food supply is an important factor in these different circumstances, suggests Macdonald, "a study of the behavior of cats from populations with contrasting diets (*e.g.* more or less dependent on human provisioning) may show the limits within which cat society varies and explain why it varies the way it does."

We are a long way from understanding these limits, or even knowing whether the food supply is the most important way to define the circumstances. Population density, for instance, is another contender. But like a family doing a jigsaw puzzle together (without the cover of the box as a guide), some researchers are working on what may turn out to be edges and some are working on what may turn out to be discrete areas in the middle. When the picture appears, we may be surprised, or we may feel we have known it all along. Perhaps we have been looking at key pieces all along, not registering what we see.

A detailed—and extraordinary—piece of the picture comes out of Devon, out of the work done by David Macdonald and Peter Apps. They call their Devon cats "semi-independent" in terms of food, and thus intermediate between the "independent" cats of the Monach Islands and the "totally dependent" cats of the Portsmouth dockyard. At the start of the research in 1977, the colony included a pair (Tom and Smudge) and their two female offspring (Pickle and Domino). Intensive observations showed the four to be "very sociable," with "amicable interactions" all the way around and with frequent changes in the pattern of these interactions. Pickle and Domino, for instance, increased their friendly attentions to each other after they lost their litters simultaneously to cat flu.

Cooperative behavior was evident. "Mothers frequently reared their kittens communally, sharing the same lair and suckling and guarding each other's kittens." Pickle even helped to sever an umbilical cord as Domino was giving birth. "Since all the cats in the colony are relatives," says Macdonald, "this behavior is compatible with the theory of kin selection" (an individual furthering its own genes by favoring relatives who aren't offspring). "However, the collaboration may also be explained as an example of reciprocal altruism (each female benefitting from the others' assistance irrespective of their genetic relationship)."

The cats were often physically close; a cat was touching another cat "roughly half" the times it was seen sleeping or sitting motionless. The cats showed very little aggression toward each other. Of approximately twelve hundred recorded interactions, only seventy-two could be called "aggressive encounters," and only thirty-six of these could be called serious. *All* of the serious aggressive encounters were aimed at a "stray subadult male."

These cats are undeniably a social group, "an amicable community that excludes strangers and within which various stable relationships exist," say Macdonald and Apps. The necessary relocation of the cats to another farm in 1979 "had no apparent effect on their social relationships," and the group (enlarged by successive generations of kittens) continues to be monitored.

Amicable and even cooperative behavior—among animals long supposed to be "asocial"—is especially intriguing. In upstate New York, Tom Wolski says, "I don't see it in these farm cats, mothers sharing responsibility for a litter." In London, however, Roger Tabor has seen cross-suckling in urban feral cats when the mothers were not even related but who "no doubt believed they were of the same family unit" because they'd been put together as kittens.

On tiny Dassen Island, off the west coast of South Africa, Peter Apps tells me he has seen several kinds of cooperative behavior among the feral cats: "groups of newly independent kittens foraging together, fostering of kittens by females with families of their own, friendly relationships between adult males and kittens, and baby-sitting of young kittens by older siblings." Apps is curious about the reasons for this behavior. "The scavenging groups, kitten fostering, and male-juvenile relationships were particularly interesting since they cannot be easily explained by kin selection." By a process of elimination, he offers the "you scratch my back and I'll scratch yours" of reciprocal altruism. "To confirm or negate this would need a longer period of study than I was able to spend on the island."

The extent of cooperative behavior among feral and free-ranging domestic cats—and the meaning of this behavior—will surely be a subject of keen attention in the years ahead. It is interesting that Edward O. Wilson's all-encompassing *Sociobiology* considers animal behavior "almost devoid" of reciprocal altruism: "Almost the only exceptions I know occur just where one would most expect to find them—in the more intelligent monkeys . . . and in the anthropoid apes." (The book also mentions that African wild dogs and wolves "beg food from one another in a reciprocal manner.") Perhaps the reason for so little reciprocal altruism in animals, suggests Wilson, is that "relationships are not sufficiently enduring, or memories of personal behavior reliable enough, to permit the highly personal contracts associated with the more human forms of reciprocal altruism." Are we now to find that *cats* are capable of this behavior with each other?

Many basic questions remain to be answered. Why indeed do cats form groups at all? David Macdonald observes that group size varies widely, as does the size of home range, "but the relationship between these two social parameters is not simple. . . . It seems probable that home-range size reflects food availability and distribution, but what factors might favor formation of groups of cats is unclear." He cites some possible selective pressures in the behavior noted in Devon: "cooperative defense of a food source, communal suckling and guarding of kittens and provision of food to a nursing mother." But, he notes, "Different advantages to sociability probably arise in different habitats; for instance, van Aarde suggests a thermoregulatory benefit for cats sleeping together on a sub-Antarctic island."

Is there, in fact, "an apparent upper bound" in the size of a group, as Robert Fagen suggests? "We may not yet be able to explain why these figures should be closer to ten cats in some circumstances and twenty in others, but we should in the future be able to hazard some preliminary guesses as to why the upper limit on domestic cat group size in naturalistic environments should be closer to ten than to one hundred." Replying to my questions, Fagen says, "I suppose the upper bound is determined by different factors in different places." It might be food in one case, or safe nests for kittens in another, or other possibilities entirely. As Fagen suggests, it is "a complex question with no easy answers."

The research on many subjects is skimpy. One of Leyhausen's most tantalizing observations has yet to be investigated (or even noted) by others. In 1965 he wrote about "something which I can only describe as a social gathering. Males and females come to a meeting-place adjacent to or situated within the fringe of their territories and just sit around. . . . They sit, not far apart—two to five yards or even less—some individuals even in actual contact, sometimes licking and grooming each other." Leyhausen has seen these meetings "particularly well and on many occasions in the Paris population." The gatherings last for hours, sometimes all night. They have "no connection with the mating season," Leyhausen stresses, although the all-night gatherings may be a "forewarning" of the mating season. "There can be no doubt that these meetings were on a friendly, sociable footing, although members of these same populations could at other times be seen chasing each other wildly and even fighting. Indeed, such an urge for social 'togetherness' exists also in those wild species in which, according to all available observations, mutual repulsion is much stronger than it is in domestic cats."

Much remains to be learned. Peter Apps tells me that the "overall aim" of his recent research on Dassen Island was to see how the cats "had adapted their behavior to cope with the unusual conditions on the island—a super-abundance of almost everything except space and water." He will be publishing detailed results before long (undoubtedly in very obscure journals). We can hope, with Apps, that the cat population on Dassen Island will continue to be monitored; for one thing, according to Apps, "the social system may change in interesting ways as cat density increases."

We can hope, too, that Paul Leyhausen—newly retired—will soon launch his investigation of the feral cats of Munich. The investigation will be on a fairly large scale, he tells me, and will depend on whether enough helpers can be recruited from the University.

We are only at the beginning. In terms of the jigsaw puzzle, we may not even have all the pieces turned right side up. But already we see the broad outline of an animal that is social beyond our imaginings—and social beyond our company.

Turtle,

who wouldn't leave

A feral cat is not issued a birth certificate, but we know the time and place of Turtle's birth, even though we didn't meet her until much later. Long ago, Roy had seen a chubby tortoiseshell kitten trotting along behind its mother; the domestic parade was making its way from the blackberry thicket just south of the driveway to the pine trees just north of the driveway. Roy couldn't remember, from that brief glimpse, whether the procession had included three or four tiny kittens. Only the tortoiseshell was memorable. We couldn't know, therefore, whether we saw the others again. But when a tortoiseshell approximately one year old turned up on the deck approximately one year later, it could only be the same one. She could only have been born in the wild. This has always been her place.

She has stayed on this hillside, outlasting the Honey Puss and Herbert and No-Name and Sylvester and her own babies. Year by year she has grown more trusting. This is Turtle's story, as much as we know of it.

Two years ago, when she had us finally to herself, we began to build a new connection. We became newly aware of her presence (and absence) and her ways. And she began to change her ways. She would let us hold her paw; she would roll over to expose her lovely white belly; she would fall over onto her back with a thud, inviting us to play with her. Most fetchingly, she would drool, back again in the security of her kittenhood. I caught a drop of her saliva once and carried the viscous treasure to Roy. It had kept its droplet shape on my hand.

She began to talk to us, with the clear assumption (I am sure) that we would know what she was saying. And we did, I think. We discerned some meows that were greeting, anticipation, response, inquiry, entreaty—and others that were complaint, demand, anger, disappointment, resignation. She had a special up-close meow that would halt in mid-meow as soon as one of us would reach out to touch her. She had a long-distance meow that would come to us from the weeds when, after a day or two away, we would return home and call to her; we would call, and she would respond, again and again, during the few minutes it took her to reach the deck and leap onto it. Are cats subtle and inscrutable? If so, no one ever told Turtle, who has always been totally unsubtle and almost totally scrutable. With few exceptions, she has known exactly what she wants and when she wants it (and that time is always *now*). Some of our city friends live with cats who are silent and aloof. Turtle is not silent, and even asleep she is not aloof.

She soon discovered the lap, or rather the five or six varieties of lap possible in a household of two people. A deep chair gives a deep lap, and a straight-backed chair gives a lesser lap. Kneeling, too, we offered a fair-sized lap. She had a favorite porch chair for Roy's lap, but she'd settle for a knee. Settle for it? She'd be on it in one flowing leap.

She became a gentle companion, glad to be near us. The night that Colleen and Albert came to dinner was magical, with Turtle a full member of the group as we lingered on the deck into the summer night. She sampled one lap after another, taking part in the good exchange among us, and when the four of us said our good-nights, she trotted off into the darkness. We fed her, of course, every morning and evening. (I don't know whether we accommodated to her schedule or she accommodated to ours.) But we joked that she was putting up with the food only because it meant getting petted—and having a largesse of laps to choose from. She liked laps. She liked us. And she didn't mind the food.

She brought her own food, too. We would often find drying on the deck the tiny mouse part she had left uneaten: a green gizzardy thing. More than once we saw her bring the entire rodent onto the deck, sometimes trotting with it from a good distance, meowing through the dead mouse that dangled over each side of her mouth like a moustache. "This is her home," said Roy. "Of course she'd bring her mice here." But if she simply wanted peace and quiet for her brief meal (a small vole is gone in a minute or so), she could have eaten it anywhere nearby. No, she needed to have us *see* it, and so we played our part as we suspected she wanted it played. We exclaimed over the catch so that she would know we'd seen it; if we had been her kittens, and the prey still alive (as occasionally it was), she would know we'd learned the lesson.

She went off to her own place at night, but she became increasingly interested in our place, or perhaps just in us. I was sitting at the kitchen table one day, wondering whether Turtle might be near, and I must have glanced over to the door leading to the deck. There she was, at precisely the point on the deck where she could look through the glass in the door and see me—and I could look through the glass and see her.

Then she found me in my office, which is on the second floor and looks over the carport and up the hillside. Many times I would put down my work for a moment to gaze out at the hillside, and I would see Turtle staring at me through the window, the dear crooked little face and the golden eyes not four feet from my own face. Often I heard her talking to me before I saw her.

We were having a new wing constructed, and she found another route to my place one evening, staring at me through another window of my office. Her muddy paw prints were visible the next day on the roofing paper; from my window, the trail led across the roof of the new wing to the builder's ladder at the edge of the roof. Impressive!

As that autumn waned, and as construction progressed on the new wing, she built several "houses" in it for herself. She made a little nest by clawing down some pink insulation from between the studs. She left this for a more luxurious place in a large open package of the insulation; she settled into the carton of fluff, barely lifting her head to greet us when we came looking for her.

But the new wing was soon enclosed, and Turtle was again fully outside. What would she make of the *inside* of the house? Not a couple of rooms under construction, but the house itself, fully furnished. The next time she looked in at my desk, Roy opened the window screen, waited for her to climb inside, and carried her downstairs. He put her down in the living room. She was purring loudly. She walked through the room quickly, exploring and sniffing. She poked into all the little places: a cupboard, the bottom of a small bookshelf. She seemed oblivious to us, and indeed we were as dumb as chairs. After a few moments—fascinating to all three of us—Roy took her outside. Later that day, she was sitting near him on the deck; when he got up and moved toward the kitchen, she reached the door ahead of him and scrambled inside. Again she explored, and again he took her out.

We had decided to try to bring her in. She must have known it. But Roy was getting injections to counteract his allergy to cats and wasn't ready for her yet. A few weeks later, when I returned home from a trip of several days, she was at the kitchen door fifteen minutes after my return; Roy opened the door, and she pushed past him into the kitchen, heading straight for me. No house explorations this time. She jumped into my lap, readjusted her weight a couple of times, and drooled. She *missed* me! She missed *me!* I was ready to share the house with her.

Over the next few weeks, we had her inside the house a number of times, putting her outside (rather unceremoniously) after a few hours. She liked being where we were, in the house, or where we had been. She discovered our bed and was happy settling into any garment we might have left on the comforter. And she liked being by herself. She found a place on the brown couch downstairs, on a pillow that molded itself to her shape.

But now we had a problem. We had a shiny yellow litter box and a ten-pound bag of litter, and we had a cat who had grown up in the woods. Roy set her down in the litter box a few times and tried to leave her there alone, but she trotted after him. One day he found a scat in the driveway and carried it to the litter box in a paper towel, but she sniffed at it, shrugged, and padded upstairs to our bed. (Yes, she shrugged: "Turtle is the only cat I can see shrugging," said Roy.) We were baffled about what to do next, and we wondered whether Turtle was also baffled. We began looking in odd corners for a telltale lump or puddle; we began sniffing for a telltale odor. Nothing. At least she hadn't decided to use the gravel bed under the wood stove. This would have made a huge and dreadful litter box; the rectangle is about four feet by six feet, to protect the floor under and around the stove.

Then we thought of putting Turtle and the litter box into the bathroom overnight. But she was new to the house, and it didn't seem sensible or decent to confine her. She was now spending nights inside, mostly on our bed, and we were letting her find the places she liked best.

So, for most of October, she was in the house whenever she pleased, and she went out whenever she marched us to the kitchen door. (She got back in again whenever she and we were at the kitchen door at the same time.) And for all that time, we had a litter box with pristine litter. We relied on her leaving her wastes outside during her time there, and sometimes she was brief and to the point: after one supper, she trotted over to the kitchen door, meowed it open, scooted off some twenty feet, left her droppings, and bounded up to the deck again—all in less than five minutes.

But what about bad weather? What about winter? That would be asking for a lot of control from her, and a lot of coordination from us at the kitchen door. Before we got really worried, though, she got the idea. She simply used the litter box. She had been restless one morning and had gone downstairs at about six o'clock. Later, when we prodded the disarranged granules with a long spoon, we found a substantial wetness. She used the box again that day. She had been outside, and when I opened the kitchen door, she marched straight for the litter box, two rooms away, and left several good-sized scats neatly buried. Thus was it learned! I wouldn't say she had been "well-behaved" not to leave anything on the bed, on the floor, under the stove, or in any number of more remote places. Hardly. She must have felt instinctively that it wasn't safe to leave anything unburied there. And she just took her time figuring out the rest of it. Naturally, we thought her wondrously clever and told her so with great frequency.

But she seemed different now. When she was living in the wild, I was enchanted by her "tameness" and moved that she always wanted a lap. Now, indoors, she kept to herself and slept a great deal. She didn't drool anymore. She had changed and I was disappointed. What had I expected? Gratitude? Mental development? Be realistic, I scolded myself. Be glad for what she is, not sorry for what she isn't. She was trusting, asleep on her back on the bed, her feet stretched out at all angles. She heard us approaching but didn't shift position. She trusted us. Let her sleep.

And then we discovered the lump in her abdomen. We took her to Dr. Glanzberg, who had seen her several months earlier for shots and an annual checkup; at that time he had thought her uterus was slightly enlarged, but he hadn't felt any kittens inside. Possibly she'd been spayed by someone, he thought then. She wasn't middle-aged, as we had imagined. He placed her age at only four or five, which put her on the hillside as a kitten when Roy first saw her.

Glanzberg wanted to open her up, as the only way to explore the mass in her belly, and so we brought her back in several days. We would talk after the surgery, the next morning. I don't remember the details of our anguish, but it was a long morning until we talked with him. "She's fine!" he said. Were those his words? He'd have the full story for us when we picked her up the following day.

"It's a very unusual situation," he began. "She had one kidney missing, and no uterine horn on that side. Since the urinary and genital systems develop together, it's likely that it's a congenital defect. Also, though, the spleen was in six or eight pieces, and scarred, suggesting trauma. No telling what happened." He had removed an ovary as large as if it were a uterine horn filled with kittens. He would send the ovary for a pathology report, along with some tissue from the fluid-filled uterus. He gave us an envelope of pills for "Turtle Berkeley" and a drugstore prescription for "Berkeley cat." She'll be *fine*, he said. He seemed to know how much we cared about her. We were grateful for his kindness and his competence, in equal parts, and we took her home.

She tottered in her grogginess and finally found a place to lie down on the doormat inside the kitchen door. Did she want to get as far away from us as possible? Did she want the fresh air? I put my down-filled jacket between her and the draft.

By the next day she was enormously better. She walked without stumbling, and she meowed a greeting as we approached. She was again licking herself clean; she'd had a dried-blood smell until then. She was again falling over onto her back to have her belly petted. She was purring again. The durability of the animal brought tears to Roy's eyes. She had lived through God knows what trauma, earlier in her life, and she would live through this one. She was more alert every hour. I ground up the pills into her favorite canned tuna, and we celebrated the return of her appetite. When she walked slowly to the litter box and left enough to be scratched over, we were exultant.

She had been shaved, her glorious white belly fur gone and in its place an ugly blotched skin. She looked very odd and dear: "like she's wearing tops but no bottoms," said Roy. How sweet the folds of her fatness on her shaven belly. Glanzberg took out the stitches a week later and pronounced it a fine recovery. The pathology report was back: negative on malignancy.

And now she changed again, to a liveliness and playfulness we had not seen before. She would do a boxer's dance, on her hind legs, with the streaming trailer of the asparagus fern. Near a desk or table, she would jab a paw at anything resembling a pen or pencil. She liked my desk, with its large supply of pens and pencils, and she would wreak havoc on the small line-up of those in use (never those in my mother's handsome ceramic jar). She would bat them onto the floor—one by one—and stand guard over each one as though expecting a counterattack at any moment. When there were more pens on the floor than on the desk, I would play my own game with this Havoc Maker. I would go quickly downstairs (followed by Turtle, of course). I would putter in the kitchen until she settled on the couch in the living room, and then I would sneak back upstairs to my desk, leaving Turtle asleep on the couch.

She spent a lot of time asleep. But now it was affiliative, while before her surgery it had been solitary. She would sleep on my desk, sometimes curling into my in-basket, and sometimes settling on precisely the document I might be reading from, or typing from, or writing on—there to settle her full, round body.

Most cats, I am told, sleep at the foot of a bed. Turtle sleeps often at the head, her body stretched out lengthwise like ours, her head sometimes on a corner of a pillow! (We have a king-sized bed, so there is room for all of us.) More often she is at the edge of the bed on my side, at hip level. When Roy and I are talking a lot, she crawls around me to lie between us. (When there is something seriously sexual between us, Turtle goes to the foot of the bed, to a far corner, and faces away from us.) Roy is touched when she wants his side of the bed, as she does when I am away. He suspects he is *faute de mieux* but he's pleased anyway, and then sometimes—inexplicably—he will be the favored one when I'm still here. It is hard to keep up with her. We get everything figured out, and then everything changes. And we get *that* figured out, and it all changes back again.

She is a Presence, in bed. She snores: soft little wheezings. She talks in her sleep: closed-mouth little mutterings full of expression and complaint and observation. And she is an opportunist, settling her weight against the nearest body and pushing ever closer as the chance arises. One night I felt so crowded by her opportunistic insinuations that I went downstairs to spend the rest of the night by myself on the day bed in the snuggery. She came quietly downstairs a few moments later, jumped onto the day bed, walked over my torso to a spot between me and the wall, and then began to lean against me. I was too amused to be irritated; we spent the rest of the night comfortably enough, but if the night had been two hours longer, I would have ended on the floor.

I am full of wonder at this creature of the woods who wants to be so close to us. I took a nap one afternoon on top of the comforter, and pulled the comforter around me to make a papoose of myself. She was alongside of me, and as I wrapped the comforter loosely around Turtle, too, her purring moved suddenly into high gear: it was a deep sound, rich and heavy—layers of sound, layers of contentment.

She simply wants to be with us. We were resting on the bed, listening to TV the day Reagan was shot. Roy had recently had some surgery and was still weak, so the three of us were lying down and listening to "talking heads." When the videotape of the event was aired, we moved quickly to the end of the bed to see more clearly, and Roy stood up. At this, Turtle moved to the end of the bed, too. Television means little to her—and Reagan less—but she was astonishingly interested. Because we were.

Does it seem she's a pest, too much with us? No. Even in the early morning when she leaps onto the bed to tell us she is awake (having been elsewhere in the house for most of the night), she isn't a pest. She *is* noticeable, though. She does a complete toilet, noisy around the private parts; she walks on us; she bats at the telephone in its cradle; she swats the pencil to the floor. Finally, as a ritual of last resort, she attacks the quilted plastic bureau in the corner of the bedroom. It is the only piece of furniture she has ever clawed, but she has made so thorough a job of it that tatters of plastic will drop to the floor every few days. This devastation has occurred, I should add, only because we thought we could discipline her. She was too smart for us. We thought we would yell "NO!" whenever she dug her claws into the bureau, so it took her approximately two days to recognize this as a surefire way to get us up. We are well disciplined by now, and upon hearing her claws on the bureau, one of us will begin to look alive and will call to Turtle, affecting her own innocent way, "Oh, are you *up*? I was just *thinking* about your breakfast." (She can always have dried catfood, a small bowl of which is always waiting for her, but she prefers something canned, thank you, and we are just the pushovers to get it for her.)

I shouldn't say it is impossible to discipline a cat. We have wanted her to stay off the dining table, especially during mealtimes, and she has understood—with an occasional yell from us, accompanied by a loud stamp of the foot. Even if she is on someone's lap, and food is being consumed by the owner of the lap, Turtle avoids the table. She started to step from a chair onto the table one day, and a mere look from Roy forced her down again. ("She did a double take that W. C. Fields would have been proud of," chuckled Roy.) But in the morning we have often found a bit of wispy fur or a magnificent whisker on the clean table. I said recently to Roy, "Even if she could understand me, I would never tell her we know she goes up there."

How delicious that she has different ways: off the table so properly when we are present, on the table so lawlessly when she knows she can get away with it. But what is it that sends her creeping downstairs in the middle of the night, like a thief on softest feet, and sends her charging downstairs in the morning like the very cavalry?

She is a true character, full of contradictions and inconsistencies. Her stubbornness alone could win her a place in the *Guinness Book of World Records*. "She's different from other cats," Roy says. "With other cats, when they walk over you, you push them aside and they go. But Turtle won't be pushed aside. With other cats, when you stand up, they jump off your lap. But Turtle clings. Turtle won't be dumped." She knows what she wants, and she does her best to get it. On Roy's lap she tugs at his arm until he lets her pull it toward her—then she puts her paw on his arm and puts her chin on her paw. Just so. Yet she's also easy to live with. When Roy doesn't want her on his lap, she understands his refusal and sits nearby. And if we want to sleep through our furry alarm clock, she will conclude her attack on the bureau (a few more shreds falling to the floor) and come back to bed for another half hour.

More contradictions. She complains mightily about the snow, meowing a steady stream of invective at it (and of course refusing to go out into it). But on what seems a more serious matter, my stepping on her paw one evening, she gave only a single meow of complaint. I was mortified, apologetic, heart-stung. For three days she didn't sleep beside me. But she kept her complaints to herself. And in one of her rare trips in the cat carrier, going to the vet for a checkup, she whimpered almost inaudibly several times. It was a complaint, surely, just a shade removed from self-pity, but it was not so much a cry to us as it was an expression from her, escaping almost unintentionally. These are all comments of some dissatisfaction, but she saves her loudest annoyance for the snow. Perhaps she thinks we can do something about it?

She is both smart and dumb, like most of us, I suppose. I can be working in the kitchen for thirty minutes, opening and closing the refrigerator, preparing chicken, cleaning vegetables. But when I reach into the catfood bag and drop the pellets noisily onto her plastic plate, adding a loud dollop of canned catfood, she suddenly rushes downstairs for her dinner. She knows the sound of her food. Yet it somehow isn't "food" unless I do something further to it, as she has often seen me do. So I chop at it with a knife for twenty seconds, whether it needs it or not, and only then does she follow me to her feeding spot.

She has no way of understanding Roy's singing on records, and she gives him a perplexed meow when his lap is under her and his voice is in a box across the room. (That's okay; I've never understood electricity myself.) About our more ordinary utterances, Roy thinks she's either dumb enough not to know we can talk to each other—telling each other she has been fed—or smart enough to try to get a second meal from the other one. She knows a few words in our language, and "turtle" is one of them; she trotted up to the TV expectantly when a documentary was discussing these creatures. ("Laffer" may also mean something to her; she was uncommonly interested in an otherwise abstruse discussion of economics.) But she works in other languages, too. Roy was once only *thinking* of her, although very fondly, and Turtle (who was six feet away and not even looking at him) began a deep purring. ESP? I wouldn't doubt it.

She is smart enough to be still wary. A book fell to the floor and she spun around, feet planted firmly, ready for the worst. But she toppled my entire library (loosely arranged on plank-and-brick shelving) and hardly seemed the worse for it. I, on the other hand, thought the roof had collapsed.

She isn't nervous, but she worries. She worries quite fiercely about my bathing, standing guard in the bathroom from the moment I start to fill the tub until I am safely out of it again. She worries when one of us is away. With both of us here, and one going for the mail, she disappears nonchalantly up the hillside. But with only one of us here, going for the mail, she trails all the way down the driveway, making plaintive little calls.

Occasionally we must both be away. The first time, planning ahead for Roy's trip to a distant hospital last March, we thought about leaving Turtle with the vet and decided against that place of strong smells, strange noises, and unfamiliar creatures. We thought about putting her out in the carport and decided against that, too. She would undoubtedly prefer being warm and well fed without us to being cold and hungry without us. (Leaving food in the carport would draw skunks at the very least, and who knows what else.) We worried that she might get frantic at being confined in the house, or might lose sway over her territory (but she hadn't been eager to go out during the heavy snows, and we hadn't seen other paw prints for months). So we left her in the house, with a mountain of dried food and a vast bowl of water. We came home after an unexpectedly long absence of eight days and found her unharmed and unchanged. She was happy to see us, and drooled and purred and danced her pleasure. She sat on my suitcase until I unpacked it the next day.

This is her house, too. She does almost nothing in the house that offends us. She sheds a bit, but this requires only minor attention. There is very little, altogether, that offends us about Turtle. I have relished her eating a mouse on the deck, watching her quickly consume the head and then as quickly chomp the body. It's hard to remember that these inert things were recently living—these headless little tubes with their stiff little feet. (She eats the feet, too.) Sometimes she has tried to bring a mouse inside, and there I draw the line. But it's different when she *catches* the mouse inside the house. One night when I heard a thud and a squeak, I knew she had gotten one of the tiny voles that comes into the house from time to time. Very soon afterward, I heard her quietly padding up the stairs. (Her ways will always be a source of wonder. Why, even though we are sleeping, does she not seek our praise, not bellow the kill to our attention?) And very soon after *that*, I heard the unmistakable sound of chewing—in the bedroom. Enough! I did not want this dead beastie on our bed. Turtle had moved off by then to the head of the stairs outside the bedroom, and I grabbed the moment. I picked up the tiny vole in a paper towel and carried it downstairs and outside. I heard her looking for it later on the bedroom rug, and I felt a twinge of apology. But only a twinge. I live here, too.

She isn't out much in the winter months; she backs away from the draft of an opened door, her fur and disposition ruffled. But in other seasons she is eager to get out, and as eager to come in again. She goes off for hours or for minutes, with no consistency. (Or with no consistency we can understand.) Yet on certain matters she is consistent to the point of compulsion, for reasons we surely do not understand. When we left her with two litter boxes the first time we went away, she chose to pee in one and poo in the other! It is an intriguing solution, but what was the problem? I am sorry we will never know.

Nor will we ever know why, after she has collected a lot of burrs in her coat, in the woods, she deposits all the untangled burrs in a single neat pile. Tidiness? Doubtful. However much her neck and torso may twist as she reaches to all parts, she faces forward again to drop the tiny burrs in a perfect pile. Curious.

Her physical tidiness puts our housekeeping to shame; she is always cleaner than the house. We know that the house is getting especially dirty when Turtle rolls over onto her back and comes up with particles clinging to her.

Her coat has become thicker and glossier since we have known her; the hair is fine and somewhat long, and gloriously multicolored. Her orange-and-black-and-whiteness is beautiful in our indoor place, against the warm wood-tones of the house, and exquisite in her outdoor place, where she is camouflaged for three seasons out of the four. We thought she might be a Maine Coon Cat, known for its silky, thick fur, but the vet said no, sure of his answer. "She's not big enough. She may have some Maine Coon Cat *in* her, though."

She is a large cat, however, and getting bigger. Some of her added solidity is the result of the better and steadier diet we have provided, and some of it the result of our Turtle being a cat who is a pig. We are now trying to be more careful of the health of this meatloaf with whiskers, this sausage with paws. We have all but stopped the occasional taste of yogurt, fed to her from the hand, and we have curtailed her food intake at the only place (indoors) we can exercise some supervision.

"Don't anthropomorphize her," says Roy. And then with a laugh he adds, "She hates it!" How can we know what she thinks? And yet we know what she wants, our Turtle from the wild. She wants it all: the indoors, the

outdoors, and us. As she stalks through the weeds, she exhibits all the natural cunning of her species; she is at home there. But as she curls into me on the bed, she exhibits something else natural to her, and she is at home here, too. We give her the protection and attention she must have known only in her kittenhood. She could not have found this in the wild. And she *hungers* for it. She *begs* to be picked up, meowing a particular meow until Roy bends down for her, and stopping instantly when she is cradled in his arms.

In some parts of the British Isles, it is considered a good omen when a tortoiseshell settles in the house. The tortoiseshell is special. But Turtle is special beyond all other specialness. I know it, Roy knows it, and Turtle knows that we know it.

On Possibilities

Turtle is no longer feral, of course. The British would say she's been "homed," as though she'd been a vagrant in the wild, a wanderer without a home. They would also say she's been "rehabilitated," as though she'd been a wayward creature on her own, a miscreant in need of correction. A neighbor of ours speaks of cats being "recycled," as though they were inanimate objects: so many beer cans or old newspapers to be salvaged for economic reasons. I prefer the term "redomestication." It is used frequently. It may be bulky, but it is free of burden.

Do many feral cats become redomesticated? I am told by the Animal Protection Institute that the percentage "appears to be quite small." No one thinks it is large. The initiative in any case seems to rest with the cat. Ben Day, at Vermont's Fish and Game Department, gives me a likely scenario: "I suspect a certain percentage of them finally decide there's a better way of doing things. They see the local cats living the life of Riley, and they slip into the barn as a first stage. And maybe even find their way to a house. I don't think many of them make that transition in one generation."

"Feral cats who seek help from people," according to *The Natural History of Cats*, "seem to be of two kinds: those who remain unapproachable and usually leave when they no longer need assistance, and those who appear to crave human companionship and ever so slowly come to accept it, up to a point. The first could easily be those cats who are feral from birth, the second those who have already associated to some extent with humans." Indeed, some authorities tell me that redomestication can happen *only* if the cats have been reared with human beings, or have been taken in as kittens.

"Feral cats can be rehabilitated successfully," says the Feral Cat Working Party, "but they may never be entirely tamed." They are, however, "very little trouble, apart from the initial introductory period, usually make excellent hunters, and can be rewarding to keep, provided that nothing is expected from them in the way of affection for a long time, if at all." Not everyone is even this hopeful. I have been cautioned by a California woman who runs an animal adoption agency and writes a newsletter bristling with exclamation points, "If you 'tame' a wild cat, it can only be tame with YOU!" But, as always, every situation is unique. Maurice Hornocker, the expert on mountain lions, replies to me: "Each feral cat is an individual with individual experiences, and its dependence on humans varies. Feral cats do at times become fully domesticated."

Feral cats are mavericks. Unbranded. Unowned. And, in the sense in which we have come to think of mavericks, feral cats are unbounded by customary ways. Independent. Individualistic. A feral cat may become redomesticated if it feels like it, and if it has a human being available. A cat may become feral if it feels like it, or if it has no choice.

The cat goes back and forth—into ferality and out of ferality—more easily than perhaps any other animal. "Domestication and socialization (attachment to owner) in no way limit the cat's capacity to become wild or feral," notes Michael Fox.

Is this, then, the power of the cat over us? That we have no power over *it*? That it lives with us (with our permission) because *it* wants to? This is a formidable power. There's just a hint of blackmail to it, but a great deal of sweetness, too. As Konrad Lorenz has written, "The animal that could escape and yet remains with me affords me undefinable pleasure."

The ferality of cats, in fact, may be involved in many of our strongest feelings about cats. Our admiration is excited by the self-sufficiency of the feral cat. Our unease is triggered by its predatory imperatives. Our awe is stirred by its hardiness and persistence. Our compassion is roused by its misery and suffering.

Our curiosity, too, is stimulated by the feral cat. Perhaps the domestic cat isn't so domestic after all. The feral cat—the cat—is able to exist quite well on its own, its ties with human beings as broken as yesterday's spiderweb, as fragile as today's. In the opinion of some, as Tom Wolski expresses it, "cats are not *pet* animals but *wild* animals adapted to living around people." Konrad Lorenz has written: "There is some truth in the assertion that the cat, with the exception of a few luxury breeds . . . is no domestic animal but a completely wild being."

I began this book by defining the feral cat as a domestic cat gone wild. But if the veneer of domestication is so thin as to be so easily worn off, perhaps we've got it backwards. Perhaps the cat is returning to its "proper" place when it goes feral, and perhaps the idea of "redomesticating" the feral cat is only a self-centered notion of ours: that the cat needs us. I mention this as a possibility only. I do not push it as a theory. But with research barely begun on feral cats, it seems not at all fanciful—it seems even wholly scientific—to keep an open mind.

I can hear the outcry. "What? Abandon helpless kittens?" I surely do not condone the dumping of kittens. I am far from advocating the abandonment of cats. But I find it hard to overlook the reality: that cats can survive quite well on their own without direct human aid—sometimes in astounding numbers and with extraordinary adaptability.

But just as I do not advocate dumping—emphatically, I do not—I do not for a minute urge everyone to invite a feral cat to lunch. For every feral cat that eats from your bowl, comes into your house, sleeps on your down comforter, there are many feral cats too wild to assume this life—or to have it thrust upon them. By "wild," incidentally, I do not mean ferocious or dangerous so much as shy, untamed, fearful, in the manner of all wild animals. When a fearful animal is threatened and cannot flee, it can easily become ferocious and dangerous.

Feral cats are not "pussycats." Some are already tame; some are barely tame. In any case, a relationship with a feral cat can take months, even years, to develop. One cannot go into the woods (or the streets) and come back with a feral cat, as one might go into an animal shelter and come back with a stray.

I am appalled, with Edward Ricciuti (author of *Killer Animals*), that at least ten thousand American households are believed to have lions, tigers and leopards as pets. What an imposition on these animals. What a fantasy on the part of these "pet" owners. For all I know, there may be ten thousand once-feral domestic cats in American households, and more around the world. I would only be appalled if I thought the feral cats were too wild to keep this bargain. But if they were, they wouldn't. . . .

I turn now to a more difficult subject. Turtle is beside me as I write. I will pet her occasionally as I explore this next subject. She will need it. I will need it more.

Millions of animals are "destroyed" in the U. S. by the nation's shelters: 13.5 million cats and dogs killed *per year*, according to the Humane Society of the United States. The immensity of the problem may be easier to grasp in smaller numbers. In Los Angeles, the Department of Animal Regulation destroyed 21,342 cats during the year 1978–79—and that was 82% of all cats taken in by its shelters. These were the unwanted, the unowned, the lost, the abandoned. And the feral.

This is not exclusively an urban response. I have some statistics from a small rural shelter. During a recent five-month period, the shelter cared for 341 cats, about half of them "rescued" by the shelter's small staff. ("An awful lot of those had to be live-trapped.") What became of these few hundred cats? It is a taker's market, with not enough takers. Only 50 cats were placed in new homes, only 2 were returned to owners, the rest were destroyed. Not many of the cats would have made good pets, I was told; they were too frightened of people.

Years ago it was called "lethalization work." Today it is called "putting down" or "putting to sleep" and is described as "reverence for life in its truest sense." The favored word is "euthanasia" (literally, good death). From an article in Pet Pride's *All Cats*: "It takes 40 days for a cat to starve to death. It takes two seconds to euthanize an animal with euthanol-6. Which method is the most humane?" (The answer is easy—if this is the right question.)

"Death is more merciful than a life of suffering and loneliness," says a flyer from the Fund for Animals. The statement nags at me like a True-False question on an exam, without an easy answer in either direction. Doesn't it depend on the extent of the suffering and the meaning of the loneliness? Do all of the cats dispatched by a "merciful death" require an intervention of such generous and final proportions?

The motivation for this enormous destruction is not only mercy but also fear—the fear that overpopulation among these animals is perilously close to being out of control. Spaying and neutering are by no means universal, even with public and private subsidies. (The first low-cost program offered by a municipality began in Los Angeles, in 1971.) Research on other means of reproduction control is slow and costly. And the cat is very fertile. But the warnings, like this one from a humane society, are hard to believe: "Two uncontrolled breeding cats plus all their kittens and their kittens' kittens, if none are ever neutered or spayed, in 10 years multiply to 80,399,780." The mathematics may be right, but the biology is wrong. And the pitch is somehow wrong. The message doesn't get through.

Killing all feral cats has been urged for years. Forbush, in 1916, considered it "our duty to . . . eliminate the vagrant or feral cat as we would a wolf." (We have changed our minds about the wolf, of course, and Boyce Rensberger's *The Cult of the Wild* reminds us that the lion was once considered vermin, and the fox a pest.)

We don't have extermination efforts today of the sort dreamed up in Berton Roueché's thriller—the full community participating—but we look easily upon one-at-a-time killings. The map of a western state lists the "wild house cat" as an unprotected animal, to be shot with impunity. The Fish and Game Code of another western state declares the house cat a "nongame mammal" in certain cases, to be killed if "unduly" predatory. The wildlife agency of a southern state tells me that feral cats should probably be removed "when practical." From the federal government comes this statement: "It is Fish and Wildlife Service policy not to control domestic or feral animals except in cases where they are carriers of rabies." Yet the letter has two enclosures—brochures from the same Fish and Wildlife Service urging that all "vagrant" cats be "destroyed."

In Vermont, I get a different answer from Ben Day: "We don't condone the shooting of *any* animal just for the sake of killing it. It isn't a written policy as such, but it's just one of the concepts that we as a department attempt to foster. Just because the animal's *there* doesn't mean he has to suddenly stop *being* there because you don't either understand or like what his role is. Up here, there's a kind of live-and-let-live policy toward these animals. Maybe they are shot on occasion. But I don't think anyone gives them too much thought."

A veterinarian will sometimes give it enough thought to disagree with the humane societies. "I'm dead opposed to killing these cats," says our vet.

"They're not bothering anyone. There's no harm being done, no misery being suffered. If I could find a way to *neuter* them all, I would. But I can't. I can't catch them. But I don't see any reason to round them all up and kill them."

That's Vermont, you may say—very few people, very few cats, very few problems between people and cats. How about urban areas? I asked Paul Leyhausen. He believes that the question of feral cat destruction arises mostly with urban populations. "My own experience argues against it," he tells me. He has three reasons. Where the feral cat population is large and growing, there must be good food sources (rats, human garbage, etc.), and unless these resources can be permanently removed, "the feral cat population serves a very useful purpose and should rather be encouraged than fought." In addition: "All relevant investigations so far have conclusively shown that feral cat populations alone cannot seriously diminish bird populations unless there are other conditions detrimental to the birds and their survival rate." And finally: "Feral cat populations may even serve the health of singing bird populations in such urban and other areas where the indigenous bird and egg hunting predators have been drastically reduced numerically or even extinguished, since a certain degree of predation is necessary to keep wild animal populations in good health and condition."

But what about places where the feral cat is a serious threat to some form of wildlife? On Marion Island, it is the ground-nesting seabird, protected for eons by the absence of indigenous mammalian predators, and recently threatened by a steadily increasing population of feral cats. On San Nicolas Island, it is the island fox, "unique to North America in that it is found on six of the eight Channel Islands [off Los Angeles] and nowhere else in the world," says Steven Kovach, fish and wildlife specialist working on the island. "Additionally," says Kovach, "each island harbors a uniquely different subspecies of island fox." In parts of Australia, it is a rabbit-sized mammal of the rat-kangaroo genus, in imminent danger of extinction from the combined attention of foxes and feral cats, both plentiful in the bush. On Macquarie Island, it is again the petrel, even though the primary food of these cats is the rabbit. Some 375 cats take some 56,000 rabbits a year, Jones estimates, with no apparent effect on the rabbit population. (When rabbits are scarce, as in winter when young rabbits are absent, it is the cat population that suffers.) But the cats have helped reduce the numbers of several kinds of petrels; the grey petrel is no longer breeding on Macquarie Island. Comparable situations exist on Kerguelen Island in the Indian Ocean, on the Galápagos Islands in the Pacific, on the Tasmanian Islands off the coast of Australia. And undoubtedly elsewhere, on mainland and island.

How are we to think of all this? Undeniably, the feral cat everywhere is an "exotic": an animal introduced unnaturally into an area, therefore an "alien" species. Are we to destroy all feral cats? I think not. We cannot roll back history—send home all the explorers and merchants and sailors and settlers who brought cats with them to the farthest dots in the ocean, the farthest shores of the earth. But how far back should we go in restoring an area's authenticity? (Curiously, the Willamette Valley of Oregon, where Nilsson made his study of the house cat, was the precise location of the first ring-necked pheasants introduced into the U.S., brought from China in 1882.) How can we sort out the millions of animals people have transported to new environments? How can we sort out the varied adaptations to those new environments? A computer could probably handle such a tabulation—but could *we* handle it, and could the *animals*?

Ah, but the idea of a computer is not totally absurd, suggesting as it does that any single situation has a vast number of variables, interacting variably. We already know this about feral cats. Every situation is different. Sometimes feral cats exist in such places and in such numbers—and with other animals—as to cause no problems. But sometimes the problems are severe. In critical situations we *must* intervene. We do not need to intervene everywhere, however, or intervene in the same way everywhere. Complete eradication may not be necessary even in the critical situations. Or possible. Our methods are still crude. (Those currently in use for cat control are trapping, shooting, poisoning, disease, dogs. Chemical sterilants are seen as "promising" but not yet widely tested.) Above all, we need to move cautiously. We don't always foresee the ways in which any piece of the environment connects with any other piece.

The largest control effort I am aware of was launched on Marion Island in 1977 by spraying the island with Feline Panleukopenia Virus (feline enteritis). Many cats died; many didn't. Protesting this strategy as neither effective nor humane, and reporting that Jack Russell terriers had been introduced to kill the remaining cats, the *Journal of the International Society for the Protection of Animals* suggested that the dogs "could conceivably create as great a menace" to the seabirds "as that presented by the cats in the first place." I asked Rudi van

Aarde about this. "Jack Russell terriers were never introduced to the island," he told me. "Such an act would only be that of a fool!" Three trained terriers, under his control, were taken to the island for a ten-day trial period to see of they could be if use to flush cats hiding in burrows. The dogs were not of any use, stresses van Aarde, and were taken off the island. "We never even considered introducing dogs," says van Aarde. He says that the FPV method has been extremely effective. Cat densities now appear to be 65 percent lower, and the trend continues downward. This news will probably not soothe those who misunderstood the situation with the dogs. "Control" is not an easy subject.

"Control" need not require killing at all. England and Denmark report great success in neutering whole colonies of feral cats and returning them to their original sites. The motive is humane; as Celia Hammond of Britain's Cat Action Trust expresses it, "We surely would not consider that other wild animals, such as foxes and badgers, should be put to sleep in their prime to save them the experience of growing old and dying." But the reasoning is also biologically sound. Clearing an area of feral cats may seem like progress, but unless the area is surrounded by water, it does not stay clear for long; a biological vacuum is soon filled by animals from neighboring areas.

All observations on neutered colonies are promising. Paul Rees says the cats apparently survive well and his Cheshire colony has remained "relatively constant" in size, keeping out almost all new immigrants. Roger Tabor says his London colonies have maintained their "tight family cohesiveness" and have excluded other cats even after several years. He suggests allowing a small amount of breeding, to keep a group from dying out and being replaced through the vacuum effect. (Since a couple of cats are always too wary to be caught, this can all work out very well.)

Weighing all available courses of action, the Feral Cat Working Party gives its highest recommendation to the neutering of whole colonies, "provided that their long-term welfare is ensured." Leaving feral cat colonies alone, says the FCWP, is acceptable only in isolated rural communities, and only when farmers take an interest in the health of the colony. Complete eradication is supported only when food, shelter and veterinary attention are unavailable, or when public health authorities have their reasons for removing a colony. Controlled culling is considered only a stop-gap procedure. Chemical birth control is considered not yet safe and reliable, needing further research, says the FCWP.

Feral cats are being studied by individuals, by private groups (Britain's RSPCA is the sponsor of the Feral Cat Working Party) and by governmental bodies. A board of inquiry that recently investigated all feral animals in Australia's vast Northern Territory makes only one recommendation about the feral cat: "At this time so little is known of the cat's environmental impact in the wild that the only sensible recommendation must be directed towards the further study of its biology, effect and control." But then, adds the board, "other work would claim higher priority."

Here I will end this discussion of possibilities. Feral cats have many lives, many possibilities. We will destroy some feral cats, we will bring some under our care, we will bring some into our houses. And some will keep to themselves—perhaps eating our food, perhaps finding their own. We will watch these from a distance, as they survive in hardship, or don't survive, or survive too well.

Turtle is beside me as I write. She will be here tomorrow.

Acknowledgments

I want to thank the following individuals, agencies, organizations, and publications for their generous response. I asked variously for data, articles, translations, explanations, amplifications, hunches, and leads. Invariably I got more than I anticipated. These people, of course, are in no way responsible for anything I have written.

Howard Oidick, **All Cats Magazine**, Pet Pride, Inc. □ Albert W. Franzmann, D.V.M., President, American Association of Wildlife Veterinarians □ Ed Rugenstein, Secretary/General Manager, American Cat Fanciers Association, Inc. □ Dennis J. White, Director, Animal Protection, The American Humane Association □ Judith Star, Director, American Humane Education Society □ **American Journal of Public Health** □ Gordon L. Kirkland, Jr., Secretary-Treasurer, American Society of Mammalogists □ Ruth Damlich, Public Information, American Veterinary Medical Association □ Devra G. Kleiman, Secretary, Animal Behavior Society □ Nancy Christie, Editorial Assistant, **Animal Kingdom**, New York Zoological Park □ Doug Bundock, **Animal News** □ Michael Fisher, Field Service Representative, Animal Protection Institute of America □ Lois Hogan, Animal Welfare Associates □ Linda Tyrrell, Administrative Assistant, Animal Welfare Institute □ Elaine M. Newton, Editor, **Animaldom**, Pennsylvania Society for the Prevention of Cruelty to Animals □ Peter Apps, Mammal Research Institute, University of Pretoria, Pretoria, South Africa □ Thomas O. Barnes, Supervisor, Game Branch, Wildlife Management Division, Arizona Game and Fish Department □ Dr. G.W. Johnstone, Antarctic Division, Australian Department of Science and Technology, Kingston, Tasmania, Australia □ Kristine Bak, Seattle, WA □ Muriel Beadle, Chicago, IL □ Betty Beal, Bennington, VT □ Bonnie Beaver, D.V.M., Department of Veterinary Anatomy, College of Veterinary Medicine, Texas A&M University □ Alan M. Beck, Sc.D., Director, Center for the Interaction of Animals and Society, School of Veterinary Medicine, University of Pennsylvania □ Agnes McDonald, Agent, Bennington County Humane Society, Inc., Shaftsbury, VT □ Alice M. Edwards, Executive Director, Bennington County Humane Society, Inc. □ Bennett Blumenburg, Faculty of Sciences, Lesley College, Cambridge, MA □ Janit Buccella □ Leo K. Bustad, Dean, College of Veterinary Medicine, Washington State University □ Robert D. Mallette, Nongame Wildlife Coordinator, California Department of Fish and Game □ C. Richard Calore, President, The National Cat Protection Society, Inc. □ Roger Caras □ G. Zeehandelaar, The Cat Book Center, New Rochelle, NY □ Cindy Friesen, Editorial Assistant, **Cat Fancy** □ Lorraine Buchon, Manager, Cat Meow, Boston, MA □ **Cats Magazine** □ James E. Childs □ Kappy Muenzer, President, Citizens for Animal Protection □ Helen Jones, Chairman, Citizens for Animals □ John Blauer, Marine Safety Officer, City of Newport Beach, CA □ Dell O. Clark, Vertebrate Pest Control Specialist, California Department of Food and Agriculture □ Cornell Feline Health Center, New York State College of Veterinary Medicine, Cornell University □ Benjamin Day, Director of Wildlife, Vermont Fish and Game Department □ Mary Jo Kovic, President, Defenders of Animal Rights, Inc. □ Defenders of Wildlife □ M.J. Delany, D.Sc., M.Sc., Chairman, Undergraduate School of Studies in Environmental Science, University of Bradford, England □ Lynn Densford, Managing Editor, **D.V.M.: The Newsmagazine of Veterinary Medicine** □ Dr. Randall L. Eaton, Editor, **Carnivore**, Carnivore Research Institute □ Leo M. Lobsenz, Executive Director, Elsa Wild Animal Appeal □ Giancarlo Rombaldi, National President, Ente Nazionale Protezione Animali, Rome, Italy □ Dr. Robert M. Fagen, Department of Animal Biology, School of Veterinary

Staff, Science and Education Administration, U.S. Department of Agriculture □ *Nancy E. Wiswall, D.V.M., Staff Veterinarian,* Animal and Plant Health Inspection Service, U.S. Department of Agriculture □ *C.E. Faulkner, Chief, Division of Animal Damage Control,* Fish and Wildlife Service, U.S. Department of the Interior □ *Frank G. Pugliese, Acting Director, Division of Compliance,* Bureau of Veterinary Medicine, U.S. Food and Drug Administration □ *Steven M. Teutsch, M.D., Parasitic Disease Division, Bureau of Epidemiology,* Centers for Disease Control, U.S. Public Health Service □ *Gregory L. Parham, D.V.M., Viral Diseases Division, Bureau of Epidemiology,* Centers for Disease Control, U.S. Public Health Service □ *Nanette Larsen, Information Specialist,* Utah State Division of Wildlife Resources □ *Dr. Rudi J. van Aarde, Mammal Research Institute, Department of Zoology, University of Pretoria, South Africa* □ *James D. Stewart, Staff Assistant and Coordinator,* Vermont Agency of Environmental Conservation □ *Ray Ottinger, Co-Publisher and Executive Editor, **Veterinary Medicine and Small Animal Clinician*** □ Victoria Voith, D.V.M., *School of Veterinary Medicine, University of Pennsylvania* □ *Carole D. Dunham,* Walk on the Wild Side Cat Fanciers □ *Dr. Donald J. Forrester, President,* Wildlife Disease Association □ Neil C. Wolff, *D.V.M., Founder, Association of Veterinarians for Animal Rights* □ Thomas R. Wolski, D.V.M. □ *Mary W. Matthews, Editor, **Zoogoer*** □

Finally, I want to thank four very special females. First is Sandra Crawford, whom I met in Seattle when I was teaching at the University of Washington. Her perfectionism has been an inspiration to me; her perceptiveness, a joy. Second is Alden Duer Cohen of Davis/Cohen Associates; her enthusiasm and know-how are merely extraordinary. Third is Ruth Cavin, who is the kind of editor that most writers can only dream about: tough, exacting, encouraging, permissive. Fourth, of course, is Turtle, about whom I have already said quite enough.

Bibliography

Amlaner, Charles J. Jr. and Macdonald, David W., eds. *A Handbook on Biotelemetry and Radio Tracking: Proceedings of an International Conference on Telemetry and Radio Tracking in Biology and Medicine, March 1979.* Oxford: Pergamon Press Ltd., 1980.

Anderson, G.D., and Condy, P.R. "A Note on the Feral House Cat and House Mouse on Marion Island." *South African Journal of Antarctic Research* 4 (1974), 58–61.

Bailey, Theodore N. "Social Organization in a Bobcat Population." *Journal of Wildlife Management* 38:3 (1974), 435–446.

Baldwin, James A. "The Domestic Cat, *Felis catus* L., in the Pacific Islands." *Carnivore Genetics Newsletter* 4:2 (1980), 57–66.

Baron, Alan, Stewart, C.N. and Warren, J.M. "Patterns of Social Interaction in Cats (*Felis Domestica*)." *Behaviour* 11 (1957), 56–66.

Barry, Dennis. *Woodheap Cats.* London: Peter Lunn, 1947.

Beadle, Muriel. *The Cat: A Complete Authoritative Compendium of Information about Domestic Cats.* New York: Simon and Schuster, 1977.

Beaver, Bonnie. *Veterinary Aspects of Feline Behavior.* St. Louis: C.V. Mosby Company, 1980.

Beilharz, Rolf G. "Control of Feral Animals: An Animal Welfare Viewpoint." *Trees and Victoria's Resources* 23:3 (1981), 9–12.

Berzon, David R., Farber, Robert E., Gordon, Joseph, and Kelley, Elizabeth B. "Animal Bites in a Large City—A Report on Baltimore, Maryland." *American Journal of Public Health* 62 (1972), 422–426.

Blumenberg, Bennett. "First International Conference, Domestic Cat Population Genetics and Ecology, 27 June–1 July 1978, Siracusa, Sicily, Italy." (Summary) *Carnivore* 1:3 (1978), 78–79.

———. "Feral Cats in Australia and their Inclusion in the Aboriginal Diet." *Carnivore* 2:1 (1979), 43.

Bradt, G.W. "Farm Cat as Predator." *Michigan Conservation* 18:4 (1949), 23–25.

Brody, Jane E. "Personal Health: Pets, When They Are Improperly Chosen or Cared for, Can Be a Source of Disease." *The New York Times,* May 20, 1981.

Burger, Carl. *All About Cats.* New York: Random House, 1966.

Calore, C. Richard. *In Defense of Cats.* Los Angeles: Voice of the Voiceless, 1965.

Caras, Roger. "Meet Wildlife Enemy No. 2." *National Wildlife* 11 (1973), 30–31.

———. *Dangerous to Man.* New York: Holt, Rinehart and Winston, 1975 (Second revised edition).

"Cats in Central Park Fare Well." *The New York Times,* September 6, 1976.

Chapman, Jean. *Moon-Eyes.* New York: McGraw-Hill Book Company, 1978.

Chase, Mary Ellen. *Dolly Moses: The Cat and the Clam Chowder.* New York: W.W. Norton and Company, 1964.

Chesness, Robert A., Nelson, Maynard M., and Longley, William H. "The Effect of Predator Removal on Pheasant Reproductive Success." *Journal of Wildlife Management* 32:4 (1968), 683–697.

Clutton-Brock, Juliet. *Domesticated Animals from Early Times.* Austin: University of Texas Press, and London: British Museum (Natural History), 1981.

Clymer, Susan. "Cats Gone Wild: Northern California's Feral Cats Have Learned to Live by their Wits." *Cat Fancy* 21:5 (1978), 18–23.

Cohen, Daniel. *Watchers in the Wild: The New Science of Ethology.* Boston: Little Brown and Company, 1971.

Cole, D.D. and Shafer, J.N. "A Study of Social Dominance in Cats." *Behaviour* 27:1 (1966), 39–53.

Coman, Brian J. and Brunner, Hans. "Food Habits of the Feral House Cat in Victoria." *Journal of Wildlife Management* 36:3 (1972), 848–853.

Corbett, L.K. "A Comparison of the Social

Organization and Feeding Ecology of Domestic Cats (Felis catus) in Two Contrasting Environments in Scotland." Carnivore Genetics Newsletter 3:7 (1978), 269.

Dahlgren, Robert B. "The Mourning Dove in Utah." Utah Fish and Game Bulletin 9:5 (1952), 6–8.

Dards, Jane L. "Home Ranges of Feral Cats in Portsmouth Dockyard." Carnivore Genetics Newsletter 3:7 (1978), 242–255.

——. "Habitat Utilisation by Feral Cats in Portsmouth Dockyard." In The Ecology and Control of Feral Cats: Proceedings of a Symposium held at Royal Holloway College, University of London, 23–24 September 1980. Potters Bar: The Universities Federation for Animal Welfare, 1981, 30–46.

Davies, Wally and Prentice, Ralph. "The Feral Cat in Australia." Wildlife in Australia 17:1 (1980), 20–26.

Davis, David E. "The Use of Food as a Buffer in a Predator-Prey System." Journal of Mammalogy 38:4 (1957), 466–472.

DeBoer, J.N. "Dominance Relations in Pairs of Domestic Cats." Behavioural Processes 2 (1977), 227–242.

Dilks, P.J. "Observations on the Food of Feral Cats on Campbell Island." New Zealand Journal of Ecology 2 (1979), 64–66.

Djerassi, Carl, Israel, Andrew, and Jöchle, Wolfgang. "Planned Parenthood for Pets?" Bulletin of the Atomic Scientists 29:1 (1973), 10–19.

Doucet, G. Jean, "House Cat as Predator of Snowshoe Hare." Journal of Wildlife Management 37:4 (1973), 591.

du Toit, S.H.C., van Aarde, R.J., and Steyn, A.G.W. "Sex Determination of the Feral House Cat Felis catus Using Multivariate Statistical Analyses." South African Journal of Wildlife Research 10:2 (1980), 82–87.

Eberhard, Thomas. "Food Habits of Pennsylvania House Cats." Journal of Wildlife Management 18:2 (1954), 284–286.

Elton, C.S. "The Use of Cats in Farm Rat Control." British Journal of Animal Behaviour 1 (1953), 151–155.

Errington, Paul L. "Notes on Food Habits of Southern Wisconsin House Cats." Journal of Mammalogy 17:1 (1936), 64–65.

Ewer, R.F. The Carnivores. Ithaca: Cornell University Press, 1973.

Fagan, Regina M. "Cats of Rome." Cat Fancy 24:2 (1981), 34–37.

Fagen, Robert M. "Population Structure and Social Behavior in the Domestic Cat (Felis catus)." Carnivore Genetics Newsletter 3:8 (1978), 276–281.

Fayer, R. "Toxoplasmosis Update and Public Health Implications." The Canadian Veterinary Journal 22:11 (1981), 344–352.

Fitzgerald, B.M. "Feeding Ecology of Feral House Cats in New Zealand Forest." Carnivore Genetics Newsletter 4:2 (1980), 67–71.

—— and Karl, B.J. "Foods of Feral House Cats (Felis catus L.) in Forest of the Orongorongo Valley, Wellington." New Zealand Journal of Zoology 6 (1979), 107–126.

Flower, Stan. "Animal Abandonment: A Cry from the Hedgerow." The Bennington Banner, April 4, 1980.

Forbush, Edward Howe. The Domestic Cat: Bird Killer, Mouser and Destroyer of Wildlife. (Economic Biology—Bulletin No. 2, Massachusetts State Board of Agriculture.) Boston: Wright and Potter Printing Company, 1916.

Fox, Michael W. "Influence of Domestication Upon Behaviour of Animals." The Veterinary Record 80:24 (1967), 696–702.

——. "The Behaviour of Cats." In The Behaviour of Domestic Animals. Ed. E.S.E. Hafez. London: Baillière Tindall, 1975, 410–436.

Freedman, Rollie Hart. "Lions of the Colosseum." Cat Fancy 12:6 (1969), 24–27.

Gaughran, George R.L. "Domestic Cat Predation on Short-Tailed Weasel." Journal of Mammalogy 31:3 (1950), 356.

George, William G. "Domestic Cats as Predators and Factors in Winter Shortages of Raptor Prey." The Wilson Bulletin 86:4 (1974), 384–396.

——. "Domestic Cats as Density Independent Hunters and Surplus Killers." Carnivore Genetics Newsletter 3:8 (1978), 282–287.

———— and George, Marian. "Population Densities and Ownership Patterns of Preying Cats in Rural America." Carnivore Genetics Newsletter 3:8 (1978), 317–324.

Gill, Don. "The Feral House Cat as a Predator of Varying Hares." The Canadian Field-Naturalist 89 (1975), 78–79.

Griffiths, A.O. and Brenner, Amy. "Survey of Cat and Dog Ownership in Champaign County, Illinois, 1976." Journal of the American Veterinary Medical Association 170:11 (1977), 1333–1340.

Guggisberg, C.A.W. Wild Cats of the World. New York: Taplinger Publishing Company, 1975.

Hall, Howard F. and Pelton, Michael R. "Abundance, Distribution, and Biological Characteristics of Free-Roaming House Cats in Northeastern Tennessee." Carnivore 2:1 (1979), 26–30.

Hamilton, James B., Hamilton, Ruth S., and Mestler, Gordon E. "Duration of Life and Causes of Death in Domestic Cats: Influence of Sex, Gonadectomy, and Inbreeding." Journal of Gerontology 24:4 (1969), 427–437.

Hammond, Celia. "Long Term Management of Feral Cat Colonies." In The Ecology and Control of Feral Cats: Proceedings of a Symposium held at Royal Holloway College, University of London, 23–24 September 1980. Potters Bar: The Universities Federation for Animal Welfare, 1981, 89–91.

Harrison, D.L. The Mammals of Arabia. London: Ernest Benn, Ltd., 1968.

Hart, Benjamin L. Feline Behavior: Collected Columns from Feline Practice Journal. Santa Barbara: Veterinary Practice Publishing Company, 1978.

Hart, Ernest H., and Hart, Allan H. The Complete Guide to All Cats. New York: Charles Scribner's Sons, 1980.

Hawkes, Nigel. "Practical Cats." BBC Radio Times 223:2894 (1979), 92–101.

Hessler, Edward, Tester, John R., Siniff, Donald B., and Nelson, Maynard M. "A Biotelemetry Study of Survival of Pen-Reared Pheasants Released in Selected Habitats." Journal of Wildlife Management 34:2 (1970), 267–274.

Hill-Bassing, Jennifer. "How to Handle a Stray Cat." Cat Fancy 23:6 (1980), 30–32.

Hofmann, Paul. "Rome Talks of Cats: Exodus from the City." San Francisco Chronicle. January 2, 1981.

Howard, W.E. "Amount of Food Eaten by Small Carnivores." Journal of Mammalogy 38:4 (1957), 516–517.

Hubbs, Earl L. "Food Habits of Feral House Cats in the Sacramento Valley." California Fish and Game 37 (1951), 177–189.

Jackson, Oliphant. "Problems Identified by the Feral Cat Working Party." In The Ecology and Control of Feral Cats: Proceedings of a Symposium held at Royal Holloway College, University of London, 23–24 September 1980. Potters Bar: The Universities Federation for Animal Welfare, 1981, 81–82.

Jackson, William B. "Food Habits of Baltimore, Maryland, Cats in Relation to Rat Populations." Journal of Mammalogy 32:4 (1951), 458–461.

Jacobson, Ethel. The Cats of Sea-Cliff Castle. Los Angeles: Ward Ritchie Press, 1972.

Jones, Evans. "Ecology of the Feral Cat, Felis catus (L.), (Carnivora: Felidae) on Macquarie Island." Australian Wildlife Research 4 (1977), 249–262.

————. "A Survey of Burrow-Nesting Petrels at Macquarie Island Based upon Remains Left by Predators." Notornis 27:1 (1980), 11–20.

———— and Coman, Brian J. "Ecology of the Feral Cat, Felis catus (L.), in South-Eastern Australia. I. Diet." Australian Wildlife Research 8 (1981), 537–547.

———— and Skira, I.J. "Breeding Distribution of the Great Skua at Macquarie Island in Relation to Numbers of Rabbits." The Emu 79:1 (1979), 19–23.

Joshua, Joan O. "Abnormal Behavior in Cats." In Abnormal Behavior in Animals. Ed. M.W. Fox. Philadelphia: W.B. Saunders Company, 1968.

Kellert, Stephen R. "Perceptions of Animals in American Society." *Forty-first North American Wildlife Conference*, 1976, 533–546.

Kendall, Thomas R. "Cat Population Control: Vasectomize Dominant Males." *California Veterinarian* 33:7 (1979), 9–12.

King, D.R., Oliver, A.J., and Mead, R.J. "*Bettongia* and Fluoroacetate: A Role for 1080 in Fauna Management." *Australian Wildlife Research* 8 (1981), 529–536.

Kirkpatrick, Ralph D. "Mammals of Johnston Atoll." *Journal of Mammalogy* 47:4 (1966), 728–729.

Kleiman, D.G. and Eisenberg, J.F. "Comparisons of Canid and Felid Social Systems from an Evolutionary Perspective." *Animal Behaviour* 21:4 (1973), 637–659.

Korschgen, Leroy J. "Food Habits of the Coyote in Missouri." *Journal of Wildlife Management* 21:4 (1957), 424–435.

———. *Food Habits of Coyotes, Foxes, House Cats and Bobcats in Missouri*. Jefferson City: Missouri Fish and Game Division, 1957.

Kovach, S.D. and Dow, R.J. *Ecology of the Feral Cat on San Nicolas Island, 1980*. (Technical Memorandum TM–81–29.) Point Mugu: Pacific Missile Test Center, 1981.

Kristensen, Tom. "Feral Cat Control in Denmark." In *The Ecology and Control of Feral Cats: Proceedings of a Symposium held at Royal Holloway College, University of London, 23–24 September 1980*. Potters Bar: The Universities Federation for Animal Welfare, 1981, 68–72.

Langer, Nola. *Dusty*. New York: Coward, McCann & Geoghegan, Inc., 1976.

Laundré, John. "The Daytime Behaviour of Domestic Cats in a Free-Roaming Population." *Animal Behaviour* 25 (1977), 990–998.

Leavitt, Emily Stewart. "Cats." In *Animals and Their Legal Rights: A Survey of American Laws from 1641 to 1978*. Ed. Emily Stewart Leavitt. Washington: Animal Welfare Institute, 1978 (third edition), 81–84.

Leopold, Aldo. *Report on a Game Survey of the North Central States*. Sporting Arms and Ammunition Manufacturers Institute, 1931.

Lesel, René. "Rapport sur l'État de Développement de la Population de Chat Feral (*Felis lybica* L.) aux Iles Kerguelen au 1er Janvier 1968." *Territoire des Terres Australes et Antarctiques Françaises* 55–56 (1971), 55–63.

Letts, G.A., Bassingthwaighte, A., and de Vos, W.E.L. *Feral Animals in the Northern Territory: Report of the Board of Inquiry, 1979*. Government Printer of the Northern Territory, 1979.

Leyhausen, Paul. "The Communal Organization of Solitary Mammals." *Symposium of the Zoological Society of London*, 14 (1965), 249–263. (Reprinted in *Environmental Psychology*. Ed. Proshansky et al. New York: Holt, Rinehart and Winston, Inc., 1970, 183–195.)

———. "Social Organization and Density Tolerance in Mammals." 1965. In *Motivation of Human and Animal Behavior: An Ethological View*. Lorenz, Konrad, and Leyhausen, Paul. New York: Van Nostrand Reinhold Company, 1973.

———. "Cat Family." In *Encyclopedia Americana* 5 (1978), 809–812.

———. *Cat Behavior: The Predatory and Social Behavior of Domestic and Wild Cats*. New York and London: Garland STPM Press, 1979. (Translation of *Verhaltensstudien an Katzen*, Fourth edition. Berlin and Hamburg: Verlagsbuchhandlung Paul Parey, 1975.)

Liberg, Olof. "Spacing Patterns in a Population of Rural Free Roaming Domestic Cats." *Oikos* 35 (1980), 336–349.

———. *Predation and Social Behaviour in a Population of Domestic Cat: An Evolutionary Perspective*. Ph.D. Thesis, Department of Animal Ecology, University of Lund, Sweden, 1981.

Lorenz, Konrad. *Man Meets Dog*. Harmondsworth: Penguin Books Ltd., 1964. (Originally published in Austria, 1953, as *So Kam der Mensch auf den Hund*.)

Macdonald, David W. *Rabies and Wildlife: A Biologist's Perspective*. New York and Oxford: Oxford University Press, 1980.

———. "The Behaviour and Ecology of Farm Cats." In *The Ecology and Control of Feral Cats: Proceedings of a Symposium held at Royal Hollo-*

way College, University of London, 23–24 September 1980. Potters Bar: The Universities Federation for Animal Welfare, 1981, 23–29.

———— and Apps, Peter J. "The Social Behaviour of a Group of Semi-Dependent Farm Cats, Felis catus: A Progress Report." Carnivore Genetics Newsletter 3:7 (1978), 256–268.

"Marion Island: Introduction of Feline Panleukopenia." Newsletter of the International Society for the Protection of Animals (Summer 1980), 5.

Marr, John S. and Beck, Alan M., "Rabies in New York City, with New Guidelines for Prophylaxis." Bulletin of the New York Academy of Medicine 52:5 (1976), 605–616.

Marshall, William H. "A Note on the Food Habits of Feral Cats on Little Barrier Island, New Zealand." New Zealand Journal of Science 4 (1961), 822–824.

Matheson, Colin. "The Domestic Cat as a Factor in Urban Ecology." Journal of Animal Ecology 13 (1944), 130–133.

McDonough, Susan, with Lawson, Bryna. The Complete Book of Questions Cat Owners Ask Their Vets, and Answers. Philadelphia: Running Press, 1980.

McDonald, M. "Population Control of Feral Cats Using Megestrol Acetate. The Veterinary Record 106 (1980), 129.

McKnight, Tom. Feral Livestock in Anglo-America. (University of California Publication in Geography: 16.) Berkeley and Los Angeles: University of California Press, 1964.

McMurry, Frank B. "Three Shrews, Cryptotis parva, Eaten by a Feral House Cat." Journal of Mammalogy 26:1 (1945), 94.

———— and Sperry, Charles C. "Food of Feral House Cats in Oklahoma, A Progress Report." Journal of Mammalogy 22 (1941), 185–190.

Mellen, Ida M. The Science and the Mystery of the Cat. New York: Charles Scribner's Sons, 1940.

Méry, Fernand. The Life, History and Magic of the Cat. New York: Grosset and Dunlap Publishers, 1968.

Necker, Claire. The Natural History of Cats. Cranbury: A.S. Barnes and Company, Inc., 1970.

Nicholson, Graeme. "Government Policy on Rabies Control." In The Ecology and Control of Feral Cats: Proceedings of a Symposium held at Royal Holloway College, University of London, 23–24 September 1980. Potters Bar: The Universities Federation for Animal Welfare, 1981, 50–59.

Nilsson, Nils N. The Role of the Domestic Cat in Relation to Game Birds in the Willamette Valley, Oregon. Thesis for Master of Science degree, Fish and Game Management Department, Oregon State College. Corvallis: Oregon State College, 1940.

Ohio Veterinary Medical Association. Uncontrolled and Unwanted Pets . . . A Major Public Problem: Special Report. Columbus: Ohio Veterinary Medical Association, 1977.

Oppenheimer, Elizabeth C. "Felis catus: Population Densities in an Urban Area." Carnivore Genetics Newsletter 4:2 (1980), 72–80.

Parmalee, Paul W. "Food Habits of the Feral House Cat in East-Central Texas." Journal of Wildlife Management 17:3 (1953), 375–376.

Pearson, Oliver P. "Carnivore-Mouse Predation: An Example of Its Intensity and Bioenergetics." Journal of Mammalogy 45:2 (1964), 177–188.

————. "Additional Measurements of the Impact of Carnivores on California Voles (Microtus californicus)." Journal of Mammalogy 52:1 (1971), 41–49.

"Pheasant Nesting Study." North Dakota Outdoors (August 1953), 7, 15.

Podvin, Catherine. "Butterball." Cats Magazine 37:9 (1980), 12–13, 19.

Proceedings of the National Conference on the Ecology of the Surplus Dog and Cat Problem, May 21–23, 1974, Chicago, Illinois. Conference sponsored by American Humane Association, American Kennel Club, American Veterinary Medical Association, Humane Society of the United States, Pet Food Institute.

Proceedings of the National Conference on Dog and Cat Control, February 3–5, 1976, Denver, Colo-

rado. Conference sponsored by American Humane Association, American Kennel Club, American Veterinary Medical Association, Humane Society of the United States, Pet Food Institute.

Quindlen, Anna. "About New York: Feline Aid and Comfort on West 25th Street." *The New York Times,* January 6, 1982.

Reed, J.D. "Crazy over Cats." *Time Magazine* 118: 23 (1981), 72–79.

Rees, Paul. "The Ecological Distribution of Feral Cats and the Effects of Neutering a Hospital Colony." In *The Ecology and Control of Feral Cats: Proceedings of a Symposium held at Royal Holloway College, University of London, 23–24 September, 1980.* Potters Bar: The Universities Federation for Animal Welfare, 1981, 12–22.

———. *The Ecology and Management of Feral Cat Colonies.* Ph.D. Thesis, University of Bradford, England, 1982.

Remfry, J. "Control of Feral Cat Populations by Long-Term Administration of Megestrol Acetate." *The Veterinary Record* 103 (1978), 403–404.

Remfry, Jenny. "Strategies for Control." In *The Ecology and Control of Feral Cats: Proceedings of a Symposium held at Royal Holloway College, University of London, 23–24 September 1980.* Potters Bar: The Universities Federation for Animal Welfare, 1981, 73–80.

Rensberger, Boyce. *The Cult of the Wild.* Garden City: Anchor Press/Doubleday, 1978.

Ricciuti, Edward R. *Killer Animals: The Menace of Animals in the World of Man.* New York: Walker and Company, 1976.

Rieger, Ingo. "Scent Rubbing in Carnivores." *Carnivore* 2: 1 (1979), 17–25.

Robinson, Louis. *Wild Traits in Tame Animals: Being Some Familiar Studies in Evolution.* Edinburgh and London: William Blackwood and Sons, 1897.

Robinson, Roy. "Evolution of the Domestic Cat." *Carnivore Genetics Newsletter* 4: 2 (1980), 46–56.

Rogers, Patricia. "Nell." *Cats Magazine* 37: 1 (1980), 8–9.

Rood, Ronald. *Animals Nobody Loves: The Fas-* *cinating Story of "Varmints."* Brattleboro: The Stephen Greene Press, 1971.

Roueché, Berton, *Feral.* New York: Harper and Row, 1974.

Rusch, Donald H. and Keith, Lloyd B. "Seasonal and Annual Trends in Numbers of Alberta Ruffed Grouse." *Journal of Wildlife Management* 35: 4 (1971), 803–822.

Schneider, Robert. "Observations on Overpopulation of Dogs and Cats." *Journal of the American Veterinary Medicine Association* 167: 4 (1975), 281–284.

"Small Felids and Clouded Leopards." In *Grzimek's Animal Life Encyclopedia,* 12. New York: Van Nostrand Reinhold, 1975, 286–302.

Smith, Lona A. "The Barn Cat." *Cats Magazine* 34: 11 (1977), 8–9.

Southam, Major Norman. "Health Hazards in Hospital Areas." In *The Ecology and Control of Feral Cats: Proceedings of a Symposium held at Royal Holloway College, University of London, 23–24 September 1980.* Potters Bar: The Universities Federation for Animal Welfare, 1981, 63–67.

Steele, Jim. "San Nicolas Island: Home of Indian Artifacts, Unusual Wildlife and Guided Missiles." *Outdoor California* 40: 5 (1979), 29–30.

Swails, Molly. "Wherefore Art Thou Romeo? The Life of a Roaming Tomcat." *Cat Fancy* 23: 6 (1980), 33–34.

Tabor, Roger. "General Biology of Feral Cats." In *The Ecology and Control of Feral Cats: Proceedings of a Symposium held at Royal Holloway College, University of London, 23–24 September 1980.* Potters Bar: The Universities Federation for Animal Welfare, 1981, 5–11.

Tarkington, Booth, "Gipsy." In *Lords of the Housetops.* Ed. Carl Van Vechten. New York: Knopf, 1921.

Tegner, Henry. "Wild Feral Cats." *Wildlife* 18 (1976), 78–79.

Todd, Neil B. "Cats and Commerce." *Scientific American* 237: 5 (1977), 100–107.

———. "An Ecological, Behavioral Genetic Model for the Domestication of the Cat." *Carnivore* 1: 1 (1978), 52–60.

Tomkies, Mike. *My Wilderness Wildcats.*

Garden City: Doubleday and Company, Inc., 1978.

Toner, G.C. "House Cat Predation on Small Animals." *Journal of Mammalogy* 37 (1956), 119.

Townsend, Jean. "The Plight of the Barn Cat." *Shelter Sense* 3:1 (1980), 5–6.

"Two Human Plague Cases Linked to Domestic Cats." *The New York Times*, June 13, 1981.

Universities Federation for Animal Welfare. "Feral Cats: Notes for Veterinary Surgeons." *The Veterinary Record* 108 (1981), 301–303.

van Aarde, Rudi J. "Reproduction and Population Ecology in the Feral House Cat, *Felis catus*, on Marion Island." *Carnivore Genetics Newsletter* 3:8 (1978), 288–316.

———. "The Cats of Marion Island: Friend or Foe?" *African Wildlife* 32:6 (1979), 30–32.

———. "The Diet and Feeding Behaviour of Feral Cats, *Felis catus*, at Marion Island." *South African Journal of Wildlife Research* 10:3/4 (1980), 123–128.

———. "Distribution and Density of the Feral House Cat *Felis catus* at Marion Island." *South African Journal of Antarctic Research* 9 (1979), 14–19.

Weiss, Seymour N. "The Beachcombers." *Cat Fancy* 13:4 (1970), 40–42.

"Western Australia. Feral Cats." *Wildlife in Australia* 14:2 (1977), 70.

Whelton, Clark. "What Can You Do about 50,000,000 Stray Cats and Dogs?" *Esquire* 79 (1973), 140–170.

"Wild House Cats Peril Aussie Wildlife." *Los Angeles Times*, September 29, 1976.

Wilding, Joy Frances. *Domestic Wild*. Richmond: Animal Pictorial Books, 1946.

Wilson, Edward O. *Sociobiology: The New Synthesis*. Cambridge and London: The Belknap Press of Harvard University Press, 1975.

Wolski, Thomas R. "Country Cousin: The Life of the Barnyard Cat." *Feline Health Perspectives* 1:3 (1981), 1–3.

Woodhouse, Barbara. *Talking to Animals*. Briarcliff Manor: Stein and Day, 1974.

Working Party on Feral Cats. *Feral Cats in the United Kingdom: Report of the Working Party on Feral Cats (1977–1981)*. Horsham: Royal Society for the Prevention of Cruelty to Animals, 1981.

"The World About Us: The Curious Cat." Television script. London: British Broadcasting Corporation, 1979.

Wynne-Edwards, V.C. *Animal Dispersion in Relation to Social Behaviour*. Edinburgh and London: Oliver and Boyd Ltd., 1962.

Zeuner, Frederick E. *A History of Domesticated Animals*. London: Hutchinson and Company, 1963.

Index

Abandonment, 15, 119
African wildcat, 89
Aggression, 16, 42, 100
Alaska, 17
All Cats (magazine), 120
American Cat Fanciers Association, 12
American Humane Association, The, 18
Animal Protection Institute of America,
    15, 19, 117
Animaldom (magazine), 85
Apps, Peter: Dassen Island, 70, 101, 102–103
    Devon, 43, 53, 100–101
Athens, 15
Australia, 12, 15, 17, 19, 28, 54
    food habits, 68, 69
    impact on wildlife, 72, 73, 122, 125
    See also Macquarie Island

Beadle, Muriel, 71
Beaver, Bonnie, 53, 98
Beck, Alan, 81, 83
Benefits to humans, 18, 68, 122
Biological vacuum, 124
Biotelemetry, 42
Bites, 83
Bonds with humans, 97
Breeding in the wild, 53–54
British Broadcasting Corporation (BBC),
    53, 55, 72, 99
Brunner, Hans, 12, 68, 69, 71, 73

California, 15–16, 18, 55, 71–72
    Sacramento Valley. *See* Hubbs
Campbell Island (New Zealand), 72
Canadian Veterinary Journal, 84
Caras, Roger, 25, 71, 86–87
Carnivore Genetics Research Center, 28
Cat Action Trust, 124
Cat Behavior (Leyhausen), 97
"Cat crossroads," 41–42
Cat Fancy (magazine), 25, 56
Cat ladies, 18
Cat scratch fever, 84
Cat, The (Beadle), 71
Cats (magazine), 85

Causes of ferality, 15–17
Centers for Disease Control.
    See United States
Chase, Mary Ellen, 16
Collier's Encyclopedia, 27, 87
Coman, Brian, 12, 17, 68, 69, 71, 73
Competition with other predators, 73–74
Condé, B., 74
Condition, 27–28
Control, 19, 120–124
Cooperative behavior, 100, 101
Corbett, L.K., 99
Cross-suckling, 100, 101, 102
Cruelty, 29
Cruising radius, 41
Cult of the Wild, The (Rensberger), 121

Danger to people, 81–87
Danger to pets, 85
Dangerous to Man (Caras), 86–87
Dards, Jane, 13, 27–28, 43–44, 45, 55, 99
Darwin, Charles, 28
Dassen Island (South Africa). *See* Apps
Davies, Wally, 15, 72
Day, Benjamin, 28, 117, 121
Dead-on-roads count, 25
Death, causes of, 27, 28, 29
Definition, of ferality, 11–15
Denmark, 124
Deserts, 17
Devon. *See* Macdonald
Diet. *See* Food habits *and* Predation
Dilks, P.J., 72
Diseases, feline, 27, 28, 29, 56, 85
Distemper, 29, 85
    See also Panleukopenia
*Domestic Cat: Bird Killer, Mouser and Destroyer of
    Wildlife, The* (Forbush), 66
Domestication, 14, 119
Dominance, 44, 45, 98, 99
"Drift," 55

Ecology and Control of Feral Cats, The
    (symposium), 28, 84

Ecology of the Surplus Dog and Cat Problem, The
  (conference), 14, 18
Eliot, T.S., 89
Elsa Wild Animal Appeal, 86
Emigration: of females, 44, 45
  of males, 43, 44, 45
Encyclopedia Americana, 71
Ente Nazionale Protezione Animali, 56
Eradication methods, 123
Errington, Paul, 70
European wildcats, 74, 89
Euthanasia, 87, 120
"Event recorder," 43

Fagan, Robert, 102
"Farm Cat as Predator" (Bradt), 67–68
Feral (Roueché), 85–86
Feral Cat Working Party, 16–17, 18,
  27, 118, 124–125
"Feral children," 12
Feral dogs, 12, 71
"Feral people," 12
Ferality, definition of, 11–15
Feral Livestock in Anglo-America (McKnight),
  13, 29
Fitzgerald, B.M., 15, 69, 72
Food habits, 66–74, 122
  affecting sociality, 99–100
Forbush, Edward Howe, 66–67, 121
Fox, Michael, 53, 118
Fund for Animals, The, 120
Friends of Animals, 29

Galápagos Islands (Ecuador), 123
George, Mary, 18, 57
George, William, 56, 73
Glanzberg, George, 26, 85, 109–110,
  121–122
Grand Central Terminal, 17
Great Britain, 28, 73–74, 84, 124
  colonies. *See* Rees
  Devon. *See* Macdonald
  London. *See* Tabor
  Portsmouth. *See* Dards
  Scotland. *See* Corbett
  See also Feral Cat Working Party
Group formation, 42, 43, 98, 101–102
Group size, 102

Hall, Howard, 81
Hammond, Celia, 124
Health hazards, 81–85
Hediger, H., 41
Helgoland (West Germany), 69
Hierarchy, 42
Home range, 41, 43–44, 101
Hornocker, Maurice, 25–26, 118
Hospital grounds, 17–18, 84–85
Hubbs, Earl, 54, 68, 69–70
Human provisioning, 13, 17, 18, 42, 44,
  74, 98–100
Humane Society of the United States, The,
  18, 56

Illinois, 27, 56, 66
Impact on prey, 70–72, 122–123
In Defense of Cats (Calore), 29
Inbreeding, prevention of, 43
Information, lack of, 18–19, 45, 55, 100,
  101, 102, 103
Ithaca. *See* Wolski

Jack Russell terriers, 123–124
Jackson, Oliphant, 27
Johns Hopkins University, 84
Jones, Evan: Australia, 17, 19
  Macquarie Island, 16, 54, 72, 122
*Journal of the American Veterinary Medical
  Association*, 27
*Journal of the International Society for the Protection
  of Animals*, 123

Karl, B.J., 15, 69, 72
Kerguelen Island (France), 26, 123
Killer Animals (Ricciuti), 119–120
Kin selection, 100, 101
Kovach, Steven, 122

Laundré, John, 42, 98–99
Leopold, Aldo, 41, 53, 55
Leyhausen, Paul, 41–42, 43, 44, 57, 68–69,
  74, 86, 89, 97–98, 99, 102, 103, 122
Liberg, Olof, 44–45, 74
Life expectancy, 25–27
Life stages, males, 45
Litters per year, 55
Locations, 17
London. *See* Tabor

Lorenz, Konrad, 89, 118, 119
Los Angeles, 120, 121

Macdonald, David, 99–100, 101–102
  Devon, 19, 43, 53, 55, 72, 100–101
  rabies, 82, 83
Macquarie Island (Australia), 17, 69.
  See also Jones
Maine Coon Cat, 36, 59, 116
Malnutrition, 18, 27, 28, 29, 75
Marion Island (South Africa), 17, 122.
  See also van Aarde
Massachusetts, 15, 66
Maverick cats, 118
McKnight, Tom, 13, 14, 15, 17, 18, 29,
  71, 74, 87
McMurry, Frank, 67
Michigan, 67–68
Missouri, 68
Modern Veterinary Practice (magazine), 25
Monach Islands (Scotland), 100.
  See also Corbett
Mortality: among kittens, 26–27, 55
  among juveniles and adults, 26–27
Munich, 103

National Cat Protection Society, 56
National Wildlife (magazine), 25
Natural History of Cats, The (Necker), 118
"Natural immunity," 27
Neutering of colonies, 124
New York State, 66. *See also* Wolski
  New York State Department of
  Environmental Conservation, 29, 70
New Zealand. *See* Fitzgerald *and* Karl
Nicholson, Graeme, 14, 83
Nilsson, Nils, 41, 53–54, 56, 67, 72,
  74–75, 123
North Carolina, 55–56
North Uist Island (Scotland). *See* Corbett
Numbers, 15, 16, 18, 27, 54, 55–57,
  73–74, 122

Oklahoma, 54, 67
Oregon. *See* Nilsson
Orongorongo Valley (New Zealand), 68
Ott, Richard, 81, 84

Panleukopenia, feline virus, 85, 123–124

Paris, 102
Pearson, Oliver, 71–72
Pelton, Michael, 81
Pennsylvania Society for the Prevention of
  Cruelty to Animals, 85
Pet Food Institute, 16
Pet Pride of Fairbanks, 17
Pet Pride's *All Cats* (magazine), 120
Plague, 84
Population density, 55, 100, 103
Portsmouth, 44, 100. *See also* Dards
Predation, by feral cats: on birds,
  17, 66–72, 122
  on mammals, 15, 67–72, 99, 122
Predation, on feral cats, 29, 75
Pregnancy, suppression of, 55
Prentice, Ralph, 15, 72
Prince Edward Island (South Africa), 72
Problems caused, 18, 85
Puberty, 53

Rabies, 81–83
Rabies and Wildlife (Macdonald), 82
Radio tracking, 26, 43, 44
Reciprocal altruism, 100, 101
Redomestication, 117–118
Rees, Paul, 17–18, 56, 82, 124
Rensberger, Boyce, 121
Ricciuti, Edward, 119
Robinson, Roy, 14
Rome, 18, 56
Roueché, Berton, 85–86, 121
Royal Society for the Prevention of Cruelty
  to Animals.
  See Feral Cat Working Party

Sacramento Valley (California). *See* Hubbs
Salmonellosis, 84
San Nicolas Island (United States), 26, 54,
  73, 75, 122
Scat analysis, 67, 68
Scavenging, 69, 70, 74, 99, 101
Scent-marking, 97–98
Schauenberg, P., 74
Scottish wildcats, 87, 89
Sex ratio, 45, 54–55
Social behavior, 19, 43, 97–103
Sociobiology (Wilson), 101
Solitary life, 97–99

Southam, Major Norman, 84–85
Spacing patterns, 44
Spaying and neutering, 121
Sperry, Charles, 67
Starvation, 18, 28
"Stray cat," 14
Suffering, 28–29
Sweden. *See* Liberg

Tabor, Roger, 13, 17, 28, 44, 99, 101, 124
Tarkington, Booth, 16
Tasmanian Islands (Australia), 123
Tegner, Henry, 74
Telemetry, 42
Tennessee, 19, 54, 81
Territorial behavior, 40–45
Time (magazine), 56
Todd, Neil, 14, 28, 41
Tomkies, Mike, 87, 89
Toxocariasis, 84
Toxoplasmosis, 83, 84

United States:
    Animal Welfare Act, 25

Centers for Disease Control, 82, 83, 84
Department of Agriculture, 15
Fish and Wildlife Service, 121

"Vagrant cat," 14, 41, 121
Van Aarde, Rudi, 19, 26, 53, 54, 55, 69, 72, 73, 102, 123–124
Vermont: Agency of Environmental
    Conservation, 87
    Fish and Game Department, 28, 70, 86, 117

Weight, 28, 53, 74
Wild animals, feral cats as, 14, 87, 119
Wild animals as pets, 120
Wildlife in Australia (magazine), 28
Willamette Valley (Oregon). *See* Nilsson
Wilson, Edward O., 101
Wisconsin, 67. *See also* Laundré
Wolff, Rosemarie, 41
Wolski, Tom, 26–27, 44, 55, 99, 101, 119
World Health Organization, 85
World War II, 16, 18